CHARLIE CHAPLIN

CHARLIE CHAPLIN

A Pyramid Illustrated History of the Movies

by
ROBERT F. MOSS

General Editor: **TED SENNETT**

PUBLICATIONS
NEW YORK

TO JEFF AND DONA

CHARLIE CHAPLIN
A Pyramid Illustrated History of the Movies

Pyramid edition published February 1975

ISBN 0-515-03640-4

Library of Congress Catalog Card Number:

Printed in the United States of America

Pyramid Books are published by Pyramid Communications, Inc. Its trademarks, consisting of the word "Pyramid" and the portrayal of a pyramid, are registered in the United States Patent Office.

Pyramid Communications, Inc., 919 Third Avenue, New York, N.Y. 10022

CONDITIONS OF SALE

(graphic design by anthony basile)

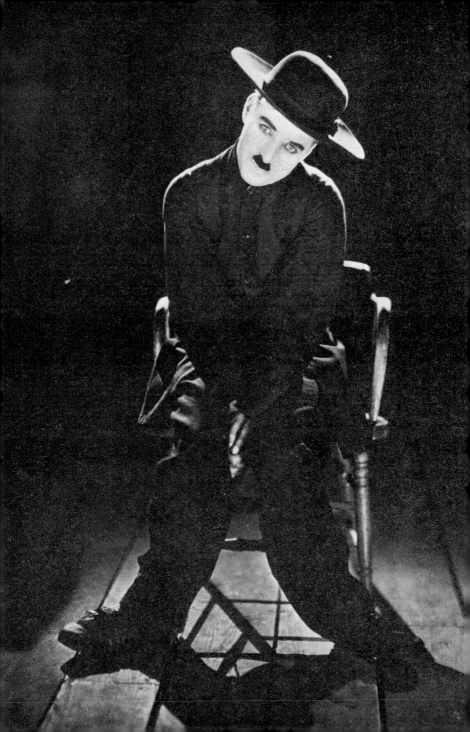

ACKNOWLEDGMENTS

I would like to acknowledge the courtesy and promptness of RBC Films of Los Angeles in providing me with prints of certain Chaplin films. I am also indebted to Bruce Davis for making his time—and a good deal of free audiovisual equipment —available to me.

Photographs: Jerry Vermilye, The Memory Shop, RBC Films, Movie Star News, and The Museum of Modern Art—Stills Collection

CONTENTS

Introduction 11

Chaplin the Man 12

The Apprentice 24

The Journeyman 43

The Master 63

Social Critic, Political Observer, Philosopher 103

Swan Song and Summing Up 129

Bibliography 149

The Films of Charlie Chaplin 150

Index 155

In English-speaking countries he is "Charlie," in France "Charlot," in Italy "Carlo," in Spain "Carlitos." These are probably the least exotic of the many names by which Charlie Chaplin has become known to mankind. But under the mask of these different labels, the figure is always the same; the irrepressible little fellow in baggy pants, constricted coat and bowler hat—the immortal Tramp. For although Chaplin played a number of different roles in his career—especially in his sound films—it is the Tramp who conquered the world with his comic and eloquent silence.

In assessing this universal appeal, Chaplin has cleverly used the Tramp's costume as a gloss on his character traits: "His little moustache? That is a symbol of vanity. His skimpy coat, his trousers so ridiculously baggy and shapeless? They are the caricature of our eccentricity, our stupidities, our clumsiness. The idea of the walking stick was perhaps my happiest inspiration, for the cane was what made me speedily known . . . with my little walking stick . . . I gave the impression of an attempt at dignity, which was exactly my aim." This vain, eccentric, affectedly dignified little man has, over the years, attracted audiences estimated at 300 million people.

Naturally an achievement of these dimensions has not lacked for interpreters and commentators.

INTRODUCTION

The first serious full-length study of Chaplin's work seems to have been Louis Delluc's *Charlie Chaplin* in 1922 and since then at least ten others have joined it on the shelf. At the same time, Chaplin the man has often moved in very different directions than his famous character, sometimes amidst extremes of popular affection and disapproval. This has caused additional confusion and turbulence in the attempts to comment intelligently on his life and work, which intersect far more often than is common among American filmmakers.

The present study is an effort to beat at least a modest path through Chaplin's long film career, trying to avoid some of the excesses—especially the over-intellectualizing and the indiscriminate praise—of many who have come before. The primary concern of the book is Chaplin's work, though a brief biographical sketch has been included and biographical elements are introduced freely where they seem relevant to the films. If there is a guiding principle behind the book, it is simply that a "universal clown," no less than an immortal playwright or composer, deserves the best a critic can muster in intelligence, taste, imagination and common sense.

In a small vaudeville theatre in London in 1894, the local soubrette, Hannah Chaplin (stage name: Lily Harley), lost her voice suddenly in the middle of a number, and the noisy, uncharitable audience drove her from the stage. In despair, she sent her five-year-old son out to replace her; unwittingly, he entertained by imitating his mother's voice cracking. The audience responded with roars of approving laughter and a shower of coins. Most of them saw the humor of the situation and perhaps a few saw the pathos. The performer was too young to appreciate either, but it is fitting that in a tragicomic atmosphere, with a warm, lucrative response from beyond the footlights, Charles Spencer Chaplin should have made his entrance into show business.

Born on April 16, 1889, the man who was destined to become one of the most famous figures of this century could not have emerged in grimmer, less promising circumstances. Chaplin's father, Charles Chaplin, Sr., a popular vaudeville singer of the period, deserted Hannah when Chaplin was a baby and died of alcoholism at the age of thirty-seven. The poverty and privation of Chaplin's youth is true-life Dickens, a saga of a penniless and hungry urchin in ragged clothing, moving through squalid streets, living in shabby garrets and the workhouse.

CHAPLIN THE MAN

Chaplin at least had a partner in much of this misery; his older brother, Sydney, Hannah's child by another marriage. By necessity, the two developed considerable resourcefulness during the frequent periods when Hannah was unable to support them. After her vocal problems forced her from the stage, she eked out a meager, inconstant income as a seamstress—this, in between the numerous mental breakdowns that kept her confined to an asylum for months at a time.

Chaplin's feelings for his mother were deep and abiding. It is not hard to see why. In addition to her selfless efforts to supply her sons with the barest essentials, she was young Charlie's constant companion and source of emotional support, his tutor and theatrical coach, drilling him thoroughly in the tricks of the stage. Nonetheless, it was Chaplin's father who initiated the boy's stage career, finding him a position with the Eight Lancashire Lads, a group of clog-dancers, when he was seven. Eventually, Chaplin graduated to legitimate theater, scoring a great success as an office boy in *Sherlock Holmes* and appearing in the first production of *Peter Pan*. He was a well-established child actor when Sydney, who had also gone on the stage, persuaded his employer, Fred Karno, to take

As a young British actor

young Charlie into his vaudeville company. Karno was one of the leading impresarios in England and during Chaplin's six years with the company, he learned hundreds of musical skits, along with the miming, mugging, acrobatics and burlesque that went into them.

It was during this period that Chaplin had his first serious romance—with a sixteen-year-old actress named Hetty Kelly. Chaplin was nineteen and far more emotionally involved than Hetty. The relationship never got beyond an adolescent passion, but it left a lasting mark on Chaplin. He was stunned on his return to Europe in 1922 to learn that this innocent idyll had ended more irrevocably than he knew: Hetty had died a short time before.

Members of the Karno Company toured America twice, and both times, Chaplin's drunk act in the sketch "A Night in an English Music Hall," caught the eye of Mack Sennett, founder of the Keystone Comedies. On the second trip, in 1913, Sennett signed the young comic to his first movie contract: $150 a week for a year, very handsome terms in those days. Out in California, however, Chaplin faced an extraordinary professional adjustment. The Karno style of humor was slow, comparatively subtle and carefully rehearsed, while the Keystone approach was fast, furious and improvisatory. Chaplin floundered for

several months, trying many different costumes, until he hit on his famous tramp outfit for a two-reeler called *Kid Auto Races at Venice*. He caught on quickly after this and was soon writing and directing his own films.

After thirty-five movies with Sennett, Chaplin was the most popular comic in the country and went on to earn huge sums at Essanay and Mutual Studios; at the latter he signed for a staggering $10,000 a week. He produced fifteen films for Essanay and twelve for Mutual, mostly two-reelers. During this heady period, Chaplin's grasp had kept pace with his reach and several of the Mutual films became silent screen classics, among them *The Immigrant* and *Easy Street*.

In 1918 Chaplin continued on his mercurial course, signing with First National in what was the most celebrated contract of that time: the comedian was to receive one million dollars for producing eight films, over which he was to have absolute artistic control. To fulfill this contract, Chaplin built his own studio on Sunset Boulevard in Los Angeles. From 1918 to 1952 every Chaplin film was produced on this lot. First National could hardly complain about this, since Chaplin's second major picture for the company was *Shoulder Arms*, which cemented his reputation as the leading box-office attraction of the day,

The formation of United Artists. In foreground (left to right):
D.W. Griffith, Mary Pickford, Charles Chaplin, and Douglas Fairbanks

while also sending the critics into a transport of admiration.

Chaplin had now reached a dizzying pinnacle of success. It is no exaggeration to say that in the post-World War I era he was the most popular and best-loved entertainer in the world. During this "Charlie craze," pirated prints of his films brought bountiful returns, and a theater in New York made a small fortune showing nothing but Chaplin pictures for nearly a decade. At the same time, renowned artists like Nijinsky, Nellie Melba and Anna Pavlova came to his studio to watch him work. His periodic hops from film company to film company culminated in the creation of his own firm, United Artists, in 1919, along with Mary Pickford, Douglas Fairbanks, and D.W. Griffith.

Naturally Chaplin's renown had its effect on his personal life. Until his success, he seems to have led a modest, even reclusive existence. With his spiraling rise to fame, the charm and ebullience that radiated from the screen began to spill over into his daily life. He entered the world of Los Angeles-based celebrities, such as British actor Beerbohm Tree (who was then making films in Hollywood) and Mrs. William K. Vanderbilt. Moving through the magic portals into the

With Lita Grey Chaplin and Elinor Glyn

spotlight, Chaplin welcomed the attentions of one and all, but celebrities in particular. This taste for fondly nuzzling the other lions stayed with Chaplin for the rest of his life.

The most unfortunate facet of Chaplin's private life was undoubtedly his marital troubles. Perhaps in eternal pursuit of Hetty Kelly, he was inexorably drawn to girls of her type—pretty, virginal, wide-eyed blondes of sixteen or seventeen. The first of these was Mildred Harris, an extra at MGM with a watchful mother nearby; Chaplin married Mildred shotgun style in 1918. It was not a marriage that had much of a chance. All his life Chaplin was as capable of moodiness as he was of congeniality, and this is the side he showed Mildred. She sued for divorce in August, 1920.

In 1921 Chaplin was able to recoup his losses from the divorce settlement with *The Kid,* which eclipsed all of his previous films in terms of critical accolades and financial rewards. Exultant and gorged with success, he went abroad for a triumphal tour. In Britain he was given a tumultuous welcome that King Arthur would have had trouble topping. The social whirlwind in which he was caught up resulted in new friendships with E.V. Lucas, H.G. Wells, and Sir James Barrie. But he also found time to return to dilapidated Pownall Terrace, where a major part of his squalid boyhood was spent and to entertain a number of his humblest fans with becoming graciousness. Then he was off to France and Germany.

The "wonderful visit" confirmed many tendencies in Chaplin: a capacity for simple kindnesses, a rather arrant celebrity-hunting, and a hunger for popular adoration. (He was frankly disappointed by the size of the crowds in Southampton.) Then, too, there was an intense money-mindedness evident in the vacuous, effusive memoir of the trip that the comedian ground out to offset expenses. This avarice coexisted side by side with the compulsion to seek out the grimiest corners of his boyhood, corners he also clung to in his films for forty years.

The year or two following Chaplin's return to America saw him involved in many different activities—building a spacious home in Beverly Hills, dating beautiful women, and bringing his mother over from England to live out her last years in comfort. With *The Pilgrim* (1922), Chaplin completed his last film for First National and was free to work for United Artists. He led off brilliantly but uncharacteristically by directing the serious drama *A Woman of Paris* (1923), a tremendous *succès d'estime*.

Shortly after this film, while Chaplin was drafting the story of

Third wife Paulette Goddard

The Gold Rush, he allowed a virtual reenactment of his experience with Mildred Harris. This time it was Lita Grey, another nubile sixteen-year-old with a mother standing guard over her "honor." Again Chaplin found himself marched unwillingly to the altar, and again the marriage was an agonizing drama of incompatible temperaments. This time, though, there were two children—Sydney and Charles, Jr.—before the inevitable estrangement and divorce.

The advent of sound in 1927 might have put Chaplin out of business, as it did to so many silent-screen performers, but instead it spurred him on to one of his masterpieces, *City Lights*, which reaffirmed his stature as a preeminent screen artist. Flushed with victory, Chaplin embarked on another grand tour—this time around the world. His reception in London was, if anything, more thunderous than the first visit. Reactivating his acquaintance with H.G. Wells and others, he soon found himself in the company of every available celebrity—George Bernard Shaw, Winston Churchill, Lloyd George, and others. This time around there was also an incident that illuminated his changeable nature. He was generous (and sentimental) enough to donate gifts to the boys' school he had attended briefly, but then too indifferent to show up and distribute them, as he had prom-ised.

After visiting the Far East, Chaplin returned to Hollywood and set to work on a new film that had been brewing in his imagination for some time—a satire on industrial "progress" to be called *Modern Times*. Naturally he needed a new protégée, and she materialized in the person of Paulette Goddard, a chorus girl he met in 1932. Though she was a divorcee in her mid-twenties, Chaplin felt that she was ideal for the part of the gamin in his new film. Released in 1936, *Modern Times* was an even more extraordinary gamble than *City Lights*. It paid off in moderate financial and critical success and ultimately became a classic.

After living together for some time, Chaplin and Goddard were married in the mid-thirties. This new wife was, by common agreement, a distinct improvement in maturity and intelligence over Chaplin's first two mates. Symbolically, she became his only leading lady in fifteen years to have a return engagement—in *The Great Dictator*. Nevertheless, the marriage disintegrated and the two parted company in 1940. Nor did *The Great Dictator* achieve the accolades and bulging cash registers Chaplin had hoped for, though it, too, has improved in standing over the years.

The forties were the low point in Chaplin's relations with his

At theater with wife Oona

public—and his government. Politically, he found himself under fire for advocating a second front in Eastern Europe and for speaking out against the deportation of composer Hans Eisler, a Communist. Not only right-wing organizations but congressmen and senators rushed to join the hysterical denunciations of Chaplin. His private life became unfavorably exposed again when he was named in a paternity suit by Joan Barry, a cast-off mistress, and brought to trial for violating the notorious Mann Act. Professionally inactive until 1947 when he brought out the unsuccessful *Monsieur Verdoux*, Chaplin had only one real consolation: his marriage in 1943 to eighteen-year-old Oona O'Neill, daughter of playwright Eugene O'Neill.

In 1952 Chaplin produced *Limelight* with Claire Bloom, a young British actress he had discovered. After a stormy American premiere, complete with a boycott by the American Legion, Chaplin and his family (he now had four children by Oona) sailed for England to attend the British premiere. In one of the more craven acts of a cowardly era, Attorney General James McGranery revoked Chaplin's reentry permit while he was on the high seas. Refusing to submit to the interrogation the government requested, Chaplin and his family settled in a handsome lakeside estate near Vevey, Switzerland.

Chaplin was next heard from in 1957 when he issued *A King in New York*, a satirical hate letter to the United States which was not distributed in this country. However, by the sixties, hostility toward Chaplin had faded in America and his films were revived with great success. In 1967 he was even able to make a new picture, *A Countess from Hong Kong*, with the backing of an American studio, Universal.

In 1972, after a twenty-year absence, Chaplin returned to America amidst exuberant fanfare. He was feted at Lincoln Center in New York, where a sign proclaimed, "Welcome Back, Charlie," and the highlight of the Academy Award ceremony was a special award to him. As he stood beaming rosily out at the wildly applauding audience, it was like a lovers' reunion.

Though Chaplin has angrily rejected most of the attention focused on his private life, he is too fascinating a subject to ignore—even if it were not the case that his films and his life are so interrelated. His basic emotional pattern seems to be one of extremely sharp contrasts. This is most obvious in his well-known fluctuations in mood, which vary from extreme gregariousness to brooding, Heathcliff-like states. As he himself has written: "I like friends as I like music, when I am in the mood."

As already noted, there is also a conflict in Chaplin between his

At the Academy Award ceremonies, 1972

compulsive acquisition of wealth and his emotional commitment to the problems of the poor. He is famous in Hollywood for driving the toughest bargains and paying the lowest salaries; on the other hand, he is even more famous for his outspoken public support for the oppressed and the impoverished and his frequent visits to poor neighborhoods.

On another plane of Chaplin's personality there is a continual tug-of-war between the artist and the popular entertainer. The man who doggedly courted the approval of intellectuals and highbrows was equally dedicated to pleasing the masses.

The last and most important of Chaplin's major personality traits—and one that is not counterbalanced in any way—is his fierce independence. No doubt the cruel insecurities and vicissitudes of his youth were the chief crucible for this remarkable self-reliance. Although he remained steadfastly loyal to certain long-time associates such as Edna Purviance, others, like publicity man Carl Robinson, were discharged summarily after long years of service. Chaplin has never been dependent on anyone. Although this individuality of Chaplin's may have its unpleasant side, it is also the explanation for the high level of artistic integrity in his works: he retained complete control of every phase of his productions. His independent spirit is further displayed in his unbending refusal to compromise his political beliefs—naïve though some of them may have been. While others buckled shamefully under pressure from McCarthyite elements, Chaplin stood firm.

Now it is the mid-seventies, and the mellow old man in Switzerland, born in 1889, has survived everything—success, failure, idolization, bad marriages, political and personal turmoil. His second adopted country—with its traditions of secreted wealth, tenacious individuality, jealously guarded liberties and multinational influences—seems like the perfect home for him. It is fitting that a life of such turbulence and soaring achievement should at last find the serenity that Charles Chaplin, who played court jester to the world for half a century, now enjoys.

"A crude mélange of rough-and-tumble," was Chaplin's description of the film series which introduced him to the cinema in 1914, the famous Keystone comedies. Their style was strictly slapstick, involving fast and furious antics, usually improvised in some familiar location: a doctor's office, a bar, a park, and the like. The staple items in these plotless, unpretentious works were violence, confusion, disaster, mistaken identities. The obsessive roughhouse was always harmless; even in an outright free-for-all no one was ever really hurt. In Keystone warfare, the most famous weapon was the pie and the tried-and-true climax was a frantic chase—an ensemble effort, hopefully involving the renowned Keystone Kops themselves. As to the technical side, a one- or two-reeler of this sort could be created in anywhere from a day to a week, at a cost of under $1,000.

This then was the world that Chaplin entered in December 1913, and it is well-known that he experienced some difficulty taking his place alongside the Keystone headliners—Mabel Normand, Ford Sterling, Fatty Arbuckle, and Mack Swain. He made his debut in *Making a Living*, playing an English bounder who impersonates a nobleman. His costume—a frock coat, silk hat and drooping moustache—was a far cry from the

THE APPRENTICE

"little Tramp." Apart from a few displays of physical dexterity (e.g., covertly snatching a coin away from another character), there was not much in this movie that augured well for Chaplin's career. In his second film, *Kid Auto Races at Venice*, the Tramp emerged, but his highjinks at the children's auto races come across as fairly ordinary clowning. It was in *Mabel's Strange Predicament*, made a few months later, that Chaplin began to find the style and form that would make the Tramp famous. The story was an energetic trifle about guests in a hotel and their ridiculous dilemmas. What one remembers, however, amidst all the knockabout humor, is Chaplin's absurd attempt to maintain his dignity in the most undignified circumstances (with his foot tangled in a leash, for example, or his hand in a spittoon). This was later an important facet of the Tramp's character.

In the subsequent thirty-two comedies he made at Keystone, Chaplin gradually filled in the outlines of his new persona, adding attributes and mannerisms as he went along. Despite their diversity, these comedies do not completely resist categorization. There are several "park" comedies, for instance, which have in common not only

MAKING A LIVING (1914). With Henry Lehrman

BETWEEN THE SHOWERS (1914). An altercation with Ford Sterling. In the background: Chester Conklin and Emma Clifton

their setting but their subject matter: romantic conflicts and misunderstandings. *Between the Showers*, which takes place on a rainy day, has Chaplin and Ford Sterling clashing over a girl and the umbrella each needs to court her, while a policeman looks on. In *Twenty Minutes of Love*, the park bench is the "parlor" where Charlie flirts with somebody else's girl, using a stolen watch as a gift. Severely harried by his enemies, he prevails by pushing everybody—cops included—into the lake. He uses the same strategy under very similar circumstances in *Recreation* and *Love Pangs*, though in the latter his rivals return to take revenge on him in a movie theater. *Getting Acquainted* is an attempt at wife swapping in the age of innocence, with Chaplin and Mack

Swain negotiating an exchange of spouses that is thwarted by a policeman.

During this period Chaplin also worked variations on the famous drunk act which he had perfected on stage. *His Favorite Pastime* was the first of these. It had Charlie creating bibulous disruptions in a bar and then following a married woman home, where he encounters the fury of her husband. On the other hand, his antagonist in *Mabel's Married Life* is a boxing dummy which his wife has set up for him; but, in his inebriated state, the dummy outslugs him. *The Round-ers* teamed Chaplin with Fatty Arbuckle as Mr. Full and Mr. Fuller, two gentlemen trying to have a riotous boys' night out.

A large percentage of Chaplin's output at Keystone was made up of comedies in which he portrayed an inept assistant of some sort. The best of these was the first, *Laughing Gas*, in which Charlie aids a dentist, Dr. Pain, with an amazing mixture of incompetence and self-interest. With most of the patients his tools are wrenches, hammers and overdoses of laughing gas, but with a pretty girl he uses a pair of forceps, gently and charmingly, to

THE FACE ON THE BARROOM FLOOR (1914). With Cecile Arnold and Vivian Edwards

HIS TRYSTING PLACE (1914). Charlie tends a baby.

steal kisses. Negligence is Charlie's chief fault in *His New Profession*, in which he so disregards his duty—pushing an invalid's wheelchair—that his employer is nearly drowned. *Dough and Dynamite*, one of the most popular of the Keystones, casts Charlie and Chester Conklin as waiters who are ordered to man the ovens when the workers go on strike. The yeasty consequences, enveloping everyone, are far from unexpected. For a change, Charlie is the boss in *His Musical Profession*, with Mack Swain as his helper in the piano-moving business; the results are no less catastrophic when he takes charge than when he follows orders.

Female impersonations and satires were two other species of humor Chaplin utilized a few times at Keystone. In *A Busy Day* he appears as an irate wife who catches her husband (Mack Swain) at an assignation with a young girl and administers a beating to the hulking brute. Chaplin switched sexes again in *The Masquerader*, where he plays a discharged actor who rejoins his company in the guise of a woman, scoring a hit until he is found out. This movie also supplied some mockery of the filmmaking process which could be construed as satire. More overtly satirical were such Keystones as *A Film Johnnie*, in which Charlie is a star-struck filmgoer who invades the Keystone studios; *The Property Man*, in which the victims of Charlie's bungling are stereotyped vaudeville acts; *The Face on the Barroom Floor*, a burlesque of the well-known poem, with Chaplin as the drunken artist; and *His Prehistoric Past*, which lampoons the then-faddish interest in Stone Age life.

A complete sorting out of Chaplin's Keystones requires a large slot for miscellaneous efforts. *Tango Tangles*, shot in a few hours in an actual dance hall, offers a rare opportunity to see Chaplin (and other Keystoners) without makeup. One of Chaplin's infrequent appearances as an aristocrat is the chief appeal of *Cruel, Cruel Love*, where he is unsuccessful in a suicide attempt over a girl. In *The Star Boarder*, there is more flirtation and another dummy, the latter being part of a practical joke played on Charlie. In *Caught in the Rain* (the first film Chaplin made entirely on his own), Charlie runs afoul of another angry husband when the man's sleepwalking wife comes to Charlie's room at night. Chaplin reverted to his first film costume, that of a seedy-looking dandy, for *Mabel at the Wheel*, in which he unscrupulously plots against female motorcyclist Mabel Normand in the big race. Mabel is again the center of attention in *The Fatal Mallet*, which is a real film buff's curiosity, since it pits Mack Sennett himself against Chaplin in a

TILLIE'S PUNCTURED ROMANCE (1914). With Marie Dressler

WORK (1915). A moment of total confusion

struggle for Mabel's favors. In *The Knockout*, an Arbuckle vehicle, Chaplin had to be satisfied with a supporting role as a referee who gets kayoed. He turned villain again in *Mabel's Busy Day*, spoiling the heroine's efforts at establishing a hot-dog concession at the racetrack. The same setting was used for *Gentlemen of Nerve*; this time Charlie steals Mabel away from Chester Conklin. *His Trysting Place*, one of the better-known Keystones, inflicts domestic duties and a jealous wife on Charlie, but he survives both.

*IN THE PARK (1915). Restrained by cop Lloyd Bacon as
Edna Purviance looks on*

A separate category must be reserved for the Chaplin Keystones that seem to be rough ancestors of his later, more sophisticated films. For example, several of the Keystone films, apparently conceived by Chaplin himself, are built around an elegant party or ball that Charlie crashes, usually disguised as someone of lofty social station. This is a device which he used again more elaborately in *The Adventurer* and *The Idle Class*. Instances include *Caught in a Cabaret* and *Her Friend the Bandit*. Similarly, the dream sequence in *His Prehistoric Past* looks forward to *Sunnyside* and *The Kid*. Even more important as a preface to Chaplin's creative future is *The New Janitor*, in which Chaplin discovered the possibility of pathos. Fired from his job, he mimes the significance of this dismissal for a father of six.

As to Chaplin's best film during his Keystone period, there is only one serious contender: *Tillie's Punctured Romance* (1914). Originally a Broadway play, it made screen history as the first full-length comedy. It was six reels long and took fourteen weeks to shoot, but its extraordinary success at the box office made the experiment seem worthwhile and other lengthy comedies followed soon after. The story is a burlesque of old-fashioned melodrama with a guileless farmer's daughter (Marie Dressler in her first movie role), a devious roué (Chaplin), his pretty accomplice (Mabel Normand) and plenty of contrivances. Fleecing Tillie of her money, Charlie abandons her heartlessly and then makes an abrupt reappearance to claim her hand when she inherits a fortune from her uncle. Life is a lavish party for the newlyweds until the supposedly dead uncle returns to claim everything. In the end, Charlie is rejected by both Tillie and his accomplice.

Bolstered by a decent narrative (and proven Broadway material) to provide structure and rhythm, the Keystoners give excellent performances. Chaplin is quite good as the suave villain, but also quite atypical. The movie belongs to Marie Dressler, gloriously absurd in her overdecorated gown and her hat with a bird on top. She wrings uproarious effects from her lumbering coquettishness in a love scene with Chaplin, her labored smiles as she tries to charm a policeman, her feverish tango at the climactic fancy-dress ball.

Chaplin's year at the Keystone studios marked his apprenticeship in the world of screen comedy and, apart from *Tillie*, it is important mostly as a prologue to his later accomplishments. Of course Chaplin's Keystone films can also be looked on as artifacts in the history of Hollywood humor. But regard-

HIS NEW JOB (1915). With Ben Turpin

less of the perspective one chooses, few people other than antiquarians and sentimentalists are apt to find much pleasure in the stock situations; the heavy, over-obvious techniques; the absence of any overall thought or design; the rather limited notion of humor as a kick in the pants or a pie in the face; the general silliness. Although slapstick later took its place in Chaplin's comic repertoire, he put it to far more imaginative use than he ever had at the Keystone Company. If we owe Sennett a debt for discovering Chaplin, we owe Chaplin a far greater debt for having outgrown Sennett—and for helping American film comedy to do so as well.

Chaplin moved to Essanay in 1915 and the slow process of emancipating himself from the Keystone style and working methods began. During the year at Essanay, he reduced the volume of his output to fourteen films, expanded the shooting schedule to a week or two, and increased the investment in each film to between $1200 and $1500. Chaplin still did not work from a fixed scenario, but he insisted on countless extra takes to get the effect he wanted. Given the artistic dedication he was now cultivating, it is disappointing that so few of the Essanay films manage to escape from the stultifying Sennett tradition.

Indeed, the various Keystone categories in which Chaplin worked the year before continued to suit his work quite well. *A Night Out*, another version of *The Rounders*, has Ben Turpin standing in for Fatty Arbuckle; the theft is compounded by elements from *Mabel's Strange Predicament*. *In the Park*, about a stolen pocketbook, finds Chaplin back among the leafy foliage, wooden benches, pretty girls and irate policemen. *The Jitney Elopement* has a wild chase, which Sennett himself might have staged, with a battalion or so of Keystone-style policemen. *By the Sea* incorporates flirtation, a drunk, and Sennett-like violence with ice cream cones. The bumbling assistant that Chaplin had portrayed in *Laughing Gas* and other films was back in *Work*, an orgy of misdirected paperhanging, and *Shanghaied*, in which Chaplin creates mayhem as the first mate on a ship and then the cook's helper. In *A Night at the Show*, Chaplin regressed to the Fred Karno routine of his vaudeville days, "A Night in an English Music Hall;" it serves mainly to diminish any sentimental feelings about that vanished institution.

At the same time, there are more significant lines of development leading out of Chaplin's Keystone period and into his Essanay films. *His New Job*, set at the "Lockstone" Studios, is a new version of *The*

THE BANK (1915). Charlie telephones as Edna Purviance holds the robber at bay.

Property Man that sharpens the satire of the earlier film at the expense of knockabout elements. Called upon to replace the leading man in a big film production, Charlie climbs into an oversized uniform and a mountainous shako and proceeds to make a shambles of the act. The object of the lampoon seems to be the gaudy costume dramas of matinee idol Francis X. Bushman. Considerably less enjoyable is Chaplin's burlesque of *Carmen*, with Chaplin as "Darn Hosiery" and Edna Purviance, an attractive blonde whom Chaplin had discovered, as Carmen. Blame is usually assigned to Essanay, which inherited the unfinished film when Chaplin left to join Mutual and added two reels of irrelevant footage with Ben Turpin cavorting among the gypsies. The meandering, sluggish work that was foisted on the public in 1915 disappointed Chaplin's fans, and he indignantly filed suit against Essanay. The only effective sequence in the film, as released, is an extended saber duel between Chaplin and a rival in which the comedian's lackadaisical poses amidst the clashing swords are strikingly similar to Danny Kaye's comic swordplay in *The Court Jester*.

The seriocomic spirit that had appeared almost embryonically in *The New Janitor* continued to grow in *The Bank* and *The Tramp*. The first of these cast him as another incompetent menial, a janitor in a bank; but this Charlie is much more wistful and dolorous than the ones in the past, a sad sack who cherishes a hopeless passion for a pretty stenographer (Edna Purviance). She scorns the flowers he leaves her, and his only satisfaction is a dream in which he rescues her from bank robbers. He awakens from his fantasy caressing a mop. Seen today, the film has one marvelously unexpected joke: Chaplin arrives at work in an almost presidential aura of dignity, self-importantly opens an elaborate safe . . . and then removes a mop. Otherwise, the film's humor is rather threadbare. Its serious dimension is well conceived, but in the execution it tends to be moony where it should be romantic and sugary where it should be poetic. Still, *The Bank* shows Chaplin's work beginning to deepen.

The same is true of *The Tramp*, the most celebrated of the films Chaplin made at Essanay. For the first time, he turned his bowler-hatted creation loose in the countryside, tagging him with the name by which he was to be known throughout the world. In the modest story, Charlie saves the farmer's daughter (Edna Purviance) from evil hobos and is hired to work on her farm. As might be expected, he bungles his barnyard duties; however, he performs a far greater ser-

THE TRAMP (1915). With farmer Fred Goodwin and farmer's daughter Edna Purviance.

vice when he foils a robbery attempt by the same hobo band. His hopes of romance with Edna are exploded, though, when a handsome suitor appears. Charlie toddles away down the road in the first of many famous shots of this kind. Even more than *The Bank*, *The Tramp* is a seminal Chaplin film. Unfortunately, the classic Chaplinesque components —tragicomedy and melodrama built around the Tramp—have led many critics to call it a classic itself. But the comedy is strictly mechanical (trying to milk a cow with its tail is as close as Chaplin gets to anything inventive), while the sadness of the Tramp's plight is so indifferently rendered as to be largely without impact.

Nearly all the films Chaplin made for Essanay were received with effulgent praise, but only one retains much of its appeal today, *The Champion*, which traces Charlie's swift rise from derelict to sparring partner of the boxing champion to champ himself. He achieves his success by the simple means of slipping a horseshoe into his glove. Although this hackneyed device automatically sinks the film below the level of Buster Keaton's *Battling Butler* and, for that matter, the boxing segment in *City Lights*, *The Champion* has a number of pleasant moments. The first scene, in which Charlie shares a frankfurter with a fastidious, dignified bulldog is pretty close to irresistible, as is Chaplin's amusing tenderness toward the pulverized sparring partners who gather while the champ works his way through to Charlie.

In addition to *Carmen*, Essanay released two bastardized Chaplins after Charlie had left the organization—*Police* (1916) and *Triple Trouble* (1918.) The first of these —two reels of mediocre horseplay about a burglar who reforms —was shot by Chaplin himself but later tampered with by Essanay, which deleted an interesting episode in a flophouse and interpolated it into *Triple Trouble*. Whatever its deficiencies, *Police* is superior to *Triple Trouble*, a haphazard mixture of materials that uses new footage, doubles and trick photography to supplement Chaplin's work.

The Essanay films, like the Keystones, were regarded by filmgoers and reviewers of the time as finished masterpieces. Today the public has long since forsaken them and they are the exclusive property of children and film historians, some of whom make exaggerated claims for them. But their primary value is clearly the glimmerings of Chaplin's future accomplishments that emanate from them. The rather aggressive, often villainous figure of the Sennett comedies becomes gentler and more passive in the Essanay period. Little by little the contexts

THE CHAMPION (1915). Leo White urges Charlie to throw the fight.

A NIGHT AT THE SHOW (1915). With seductive snake charmer May White

of the comedy begin to expand beyond parks and hotels; the crude, overemphatic Keystone style yields, occasionally, to subtlety and understatement; the standard jokes about flirtation and drunkenness are sometimes replaced by humor that surprises and delights. Above all, Chaplin was developing a legitimate character instead of a comic type—a human being with distinctive traits, peculiarities, mannerisms. "Nothing transcends personality," he says in his autobiography and the remainder of his career is a golden demonstration of this truth.

Chaplin's year-and-a-half association with Mutual, starting in 1916, represented the union of a rapidly maturing talent with working conditions that were close to optimum. Far more important than Chaplin's munificent salary were the contractual stipulations that left him free to create his own films his own way. This he did, slowing his pace to only twelve movies, all two-reelers. On these he was able to lavish an unheard-of $100,000 each, most of the money going to endless takes and retakes. In some cases, a film occupied a full month, and fifty to a hundred times as many feet were shot as were finally used in the finished product. Chaplin's work also benefited from the small stock company of actors (Edna Purviance, Eric Campbell, Henry Bergman), cameramen (R.H. Totheroh, W.C. Foster) and assistant directors (Chuck Riesner, Eddie Sutherland) he had assembled, many of whom remained with him for years. He overran by eight months the time allocated for completing his twelve films, but all this care and craftsmanship paid off handsomely on the profit-and-loss sheets and in the rapturous notices.

Nonetheless, the first two Mutuals were only half a cut above the Essanay films—workmanlike slapstick with characteristic gusto and plenty of accidents, confusion and physical punishment. In *The Floor-walker*, the peg on which the uncomplicated humor was hung was a feeble robbery scheme, plotted by the floorwalker and the manager of a department store. Blundering his way through the store, Charlie innocently crosses paths with the crooks and winds up, just as innocently, with the booty. Chased by the manager, and a minute later by the police, Charlie hampers his chances for escape by running down the "up" escalator. Finally the manager is knocked out by an elevator.

The film is largely a humdrum workout for Chaplin, hardly as ambitious as some of the better Essanays. Allowing for the Keystone framework, however, *The Floorwalker* is moderately entertaining, as in Chaplin's amusing attempt to dive into a satchel of money. More inventive is a routine in which he and the floorwalker, who are doubles, fall under the illusion that each is the other's reflection in the mirror. This, plus a miniature ballet Chaplin does to elude the manager's clutches, are the most unconventional elements in the movie.

The Fireman is as weakly plotted as *The Floorwalker*. A hapless member of the fire squad, Chaplin clashes regularly with the chief (Eric Campbell), plays checkers,

THE FIREMAN (1916). A game of checkers with fellow fireman Albert Austin.

and fails to respond to the frantic call from the owner of a burning house. Simultaneously, the father of the chief's sweetheart sets his own house ablaze to collect the insurance, not knowing that his daughter (Edna Purviance) is trapped on the third floor. Single-handedly, Chaplin demolishes most of an engine in coming to the rescue, but he does manage to save Edna. Among the movie's meager joys are the acrobatic skills Chaplin displays in hurtling about the stationhouse, his arrival in the remnants of the truck, and a mock song-and-dance number the firemen perform in front of a burning building.

Chaplin's conservative strategy in these two films paid off in terms of popular response. Feeling bolder, he next essayed a very different kind of film, The Vagabond. Here dramatic construction took precedence over pacing, and gags were sewn into the fabric of the story with some skill. Chaplin plays an itinerant violinist who wanders into a gypsy camp, where he rescues a girl who is being mistreated by the gypsies. He and the girl lead a carefree nomadic existence, until a handsome artist turns up to paint the girl's portrait. When the painting is hung in a museum, the girl is recognized as the long-lost daughter of a rich society woman. Reunited with her mother and the artist, the girl deserts Charlie, then returns to him in a sudden change of heart.

In this awkward and cliché-laden melodrama, the mature Chaplin can be seen emerging. The story is a primitive forbear of such later films as The Kid, The Circus, and City Lights. The blending of poignancy and humor, the "changeling" element, the integration of narrative and comedy, the girl's rejection of the Tramp in favor of a more conventionally heroic rival, the figure of the gamin—all these aspects of The Vagabond anticipate the more finished work that was to come. Judged on its own merits, the film is one of the better works of Chaplin's Mutual phase. Its imperfections are the sentimental and implausible Victorian plot, the synthetic happy ending, and a tasteless gag about lice in Edna's hair. But these deficiencies are more than compensated for by Chaplin's sensitive rendering of the emotional episodes and by the gleams of comic brilliance that flash out of the narrative at appropriate intervals. The perfect tone is established with the opening shot of Charlie's world-renowned feet. The floppy shoes, isolated beneath a barroom door, extend outward at a forty-five-degree angle. They are funny and shabby and sad like their owner, who (another fitting touch) plays the violin. All alone in his dolorous attempts at earning a few coins from

THE VAGABOND (1916): A mild attack of indigestion

his art, he is easily displaced by a noisy German band which is more suited to the mood and taste of the rowdies in the saloon. The effective use of such contrasts between boisterous crowds and lonely outsiders was to become one of Chaplin's specialties.

This episode has its humorous side, but Chaplin is funnier in the gypsy camp, performing "The Hungarian Goulash" for Edna as she washes her clothes. Within a few seconds, she is unconsciously scrubbing to the rhythm of the violin. Fiddling away in a feverish parody of concert-hall histrionics, Chaplin collapses into a washtub. No less amusing are his eccentric approaches to the practical problems of camping out—breaking eggs with a hammer and catching flies in his pocket, for instance. Pathos intrudes again when the girl, now smitten with the artist, is tardy in showing up for a meal Chaplin has prepared; his clumsy efforts at competing with the artist in sketching Edna are also affecting. Unable to match the painter in his own element, Charlie grows humorously hostile, a concept Chaplin used again in *The Circus.*

In *One A.M.,* Chaplin went back to pure comedy. The film is a solo number for Charlie and one of the rare occasions on which the Tramp had a vacation. Here Chaplin is a top-hatted swell who arrives home

in a highly inebriated state. He soon finds himself engaged in stark combat with various inanimate objects: stuffed animals, a pendulum, staircases, rugs, and—most memorably—a Murphy bed which he tries to unfold. After being knocked down by the pendulum, eluded by a drink on a rotating table and completely defeated by the bed, Chaplin goes to sleep in the bathtub. Unfortunately, these slapstick gags exhibit no special ingenuity of any sort. Only the taxi meter at the beginning, ringing up the bill like a slot machine, and the recalcitrant bed at the end provide some mirth.

It could be argued that *One A.M.* is intriguing as a tour de force, but no such defense can be offered for *The Count,* an undistinguished farce in the Keystone manner. Chaplin plays an inept tailor's assistant whose boss finds a party invitation in the pocket of a customer, Count B. The tailor attends, impersonating the nobleman, but is completely flustered when he encounters Charlie, who has come to see the cook. The two join forces to carry out their subterfuge and numerous complications ensue. The masquerade ends, however, when the real count arrives. In the mayhem, the tailor is nabbed and Charlie escapes.

This film is much more energetic than inventive, and there is no sen-

THE VAGABOND (1916). Poor violinist Charlie finds little response in a bar.

sibility at all. It comes to life from time to time, as in Charlie's demonstration of how to consume a watermelon and his use of a roast chicken as a football. Otherwise, *The Count* conveys the feeling of a talented entertainer reaching down, not too deeply, into a familiar bag of tricks.

There is a good deal of warmed-over material in *The Pawnshop* as well, but this work occupies a much higher plane than *The Count*. However, the reason for this hardly lies in the plot, which consists of little more than Charlie's daily joys and tribulations at his job in a pawnshop. There, he and his rival (Chester Conklin) skirmish regularly, as each seeks the favors of the owner's daughter (Edna Purviance), while avoiding the watchful eye of her father (Henry Bergman). An attempted robbery toward the end gives Charlie the chance to save the day and win his sweetheart.

Within its limitations of plot and setting, the film manages to supply an amazingly full display of Chaplin's varied gifts, though some are revealed only in snatches. They range from manual dexterity (a balancing act on top of a tottering ladder) to a dancerlike gracefulness (imperceptibly, he converts a boxing shuffle into a series of dance steps) to superb, if fragmentary pantomime (borrowing from *The New Janitor*, he uses expressive gestures to allude to his large, hungry family when the boss fires him). The cluttered hockshop also permitted Chaplin to futher explore his uneasy relationship with objects (dustmops, ropes, ladles, musical instruments, and the like.) In addition, *The Pawnshop* boasts one of the best-known comic conceits in the Chaplin canon: the dismembering of a clock which a customer has just brought in. Chaplin gives it a full diagnosis—listening to its tick with a stethoscope, surgically removing its innards, testing it with a hammer, squirting oil on its parts when they begin to squirm about on the counter. Finally he sweeps the mess into the owner's hat and hands it back to him with a definitive shake of his head.

Chaplin dropped a level or two with his next film, *Behind the Screen*, an affectionate remembrance of his Keystone days. It is intended as a burlesque of the Mack Sennett brand of slapstick, but since it is difficult to satirize comedy, the result is more pastiche than parody. Chaplin appears in one of his most frequent incarnations, the clumsy assistant. In this one he is a stagehand named David, rushing about at the bidding of his indolent boss Goliath (Mack Swain). The setting is a movie studio specializing in comedy. In the course of the film's two reels, Charlie provides his employers with plenty of this commod-

ONE A.M. (1916). Tipsy Charlie does battle with the animal-skin rugs.

ity, but mostly at their expense. Along the way, angry stagehands go on strike and an aspiring actress (Edna Purviance) shows up disguised as a boy. At the climax, an explosion causes a good deal of confusion but no particular harm.

Chaplin had long outstripped Mack Sennett at his forte, and for those with a taste for good-natured horseplay, *Behind The Screen* is middling fun. The best joke is another of Chaplin's elaborate conceits, a complete haircut and facial massage administered with the utmost professionalism and sobriety to a shaggy rug.

The Rink, Chaplin's next film for Mutual, is one of his best-known and most frequently revived two-reelers. It is mainly an excuse for increasing our awe at the comedian's versatility by showing what he could do on roller skates. We first meet him as a waiter who is forever at odds with the kitchen staff and his fellow waiters, as well as Mr. Stout, an unpleasant customer. At a nearby rink on his lunch hour, Charlie becomes Sir Cecil Seltzer, dashing aristocrat. There he encounters Mr. Stout trying in vain to ingratiate himself with a girl. Charlie spirits her out of reach and she invites him to a skating party. Through a series of coincidences worthy of a French farce, Mr. Stout's wife and an admirer of hers are also invited to the party. The resulting contretemps touches just about every variety of shock, surprise and embarrassment and precipitates a mad free-for-all on skates. Charlie escapes finally by hooking his cane on a passing car.

Much of *The Rink* is lackluster until the skating party, where inspiration takes hold. The rink is the perfect metaphor for Charlie-Sir Cecil's dream world of aristocratic smoothness and gliding gallantries; these he sprinkles with comic spicings such as Sir Cecil's "suave" mannerism of flicking cigar ashes into his hat. In another moment of gentlemanly refinement, having accidentally toppled on Mrs. Stout, he discreetly pulls down her skirt. While on his feet, Chaplin's show of agility is impressive, a combination of gymnastic and balletic poise. Indeed, the whole scene is expertly choreographed, with the principals executing solos, duets and ensemble numbers, as they stagger around the floor confronting one another in awkward, uncomfortable positions. The finale is a sprawling mass of fallen skaters.

From the innocuous charm of *The Rink*, Chaplin turned with bewildering swiftness to the weighty subject of slum life. *Easy Street* is, with *The Immigrant*, probably the most respected of the Mutual films. In addition to having the most carefully fashioned plot, it is the favorite terrain of those who like to dig for

THE COUNT (1916). With Eric Campbell and Edna Purviance

social criticism in the early Chaplin. The film opens on a mission. Converted from larceny to honesty by the mission's minister and a lovely organ player (Edna Purviance), Charlie joins the police force. He is sent to Easy Street, the toughest slum area, to do battle with a gang of hoodlums who are devastating the members of the force. He manages to defeat the chief bully (Eric Campbell) by gassing him with the lamp the bully has bent, but is also required to rescue Edna from a dope addict's lair. Accidentally injected with narcotics, he gains superhuman strength and quells a mob single-handedly. The last shot shows the reformed souls of Easy Street heading meekly for the new

THE PAWNSHOP (1916). Charlie as jack-of-all-trades in a pawnshop

mission on their block.

The film is a happy return to the slower but more organically conceived *The Vagabond* and an anticipation of the great work that lay ahead. Among the jokes that arise, without coercion or artifice, from the events of the story is a battlefield analogy used for Easy Street. In our first view of the street, policemen are being beaten (in exaggerated, slapstick style, it should be stressed) and carried out of the war zone on stretchers. The same functional quality is discernible in Chaplin's handling of a charity case Edna takes on. There are so many hungry children packed into the small room that, recognizing the hopelessness of it all, Charlie simply scatters cornflakes around barnyard-style. Curiously, two of the major gags in *Easy Street* have been drained of their humor by events Chaplin could never have predicted. Hitler's concentration camps have made it hard to laugh at any gassing incidents, while the narcotics nightmare that has gripped our society in recent years wipes out most of the comic element of drugs and drug addiction.

Attempts to dredge profound social commentary out of *Easy Street* invite sober critiques which are not especially flattering to this sociologically shallow work. It ought to be obvious from the script that the events of *Easy Street* are determined by dramatic and comic needs, not by any political philosophy. The nature of Chaplin's art dictates that the "little fellow" must tame the oppressive giants in a humorous fashion—even though in this case, he is a symbol of authority and they themselves, as slum dwellers, could be construed as the oppressed. As it happens, the real innovation in *Easy Street* is its extension of the territory in which Chaplin's comic talents could operate successfully. The quasi-realistic milieu, with its distinctly autobiographical origins, was a refreshing change from the nondescript parks, apartments, restaurants and mansions where so many of the comedian's earlier works took place.

Chaplin apparently did not want to rush too precipitately into the new type of comedy he was evolving, if *The Cure*, which followed *Easy Street*, is any indication. The spoof of health spas could not be accused of anything serious or avant-garde. Giving the Tramp another rest, Chaplin appeared in a light, sporty outfit as a drunkard who comes to a health resort armed with a trunk full of booze. Though somewhat silly, the disruptions he is able to introduce in the resort's placid routine are occasionally funny. His chief antagonist is a large, gouty man (Eric Campbell) with one foot in bandages. A pretty

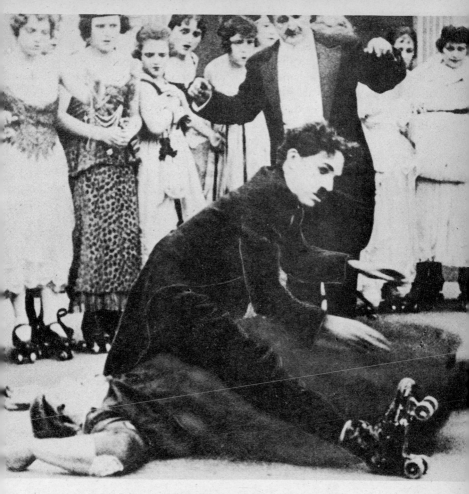

THE RINK (1916). At a skating party. Charlie falls on top of Mrs. Stout (Henry Bergman).

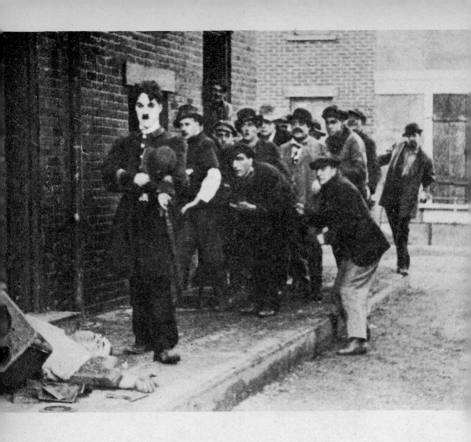

*EASY STREET (1917). Charlie triumphs over Eric Campbell—
with the help of a stove.*

but prim and teetotaling lady (Edna Purviance) is there to provide a romantic element. The climax is a mass case of inebriation when Charlie's liquor accidentally winds up in the mineral water, and the dénouement is Charlie's tumble into the springs themselves. The one bright sequence in this largely drab exercise is a wrestling match that Charlie engages in with a mountainous masseur — an uproarious pas de deux of stances and grips.

The "new" Chaplin reappeared in *The Immigrant,* one of the finest of all his short comedies. A virtually perfect melding of satire, pathos, irony, realism and standardized melodrama, *The Immigrant* was further evidence that Chaplin's genius thrived best on a subject with which he had some firsthand experience. Though he had certainly not traveled to America in steerage, he had been an immigrant and this fact, though it gave no special insight, apparently sparked his creative powers.

The Tramp is back in this one, leaning convulsively over the rail of a ship bound for the United States when we first see him. It is fishing rather than seasickness that is keeping him occupied, as it turns out. (It seems that the meals, which are none too carefully prepared, are also subject to the violent rocking of the boat.) After dinner, Chaplin wins some money in a poker game

EASY STREET (1917). With Janet Miller Sully and John Rand

THE CURE (1917). At the baths for a "water cure," Charlie has an enemy in bearded Eric Campbell.

but charitably hands it over to a young girl and her mother. When the ship docks at the Statue of Liberty and the immigrants are rudely prepared for disembarkation, Charlie loses sight of the girl; later we see him wandering the streets of New York, distraught and penniless. By chance, he is reunited with the girl in a restaurant, and they are offered a modeling job by an artist. Afterwards Charlie drags the girl, who offers some coquettish resistance, to a bureau of "marriage licenses."

As in all the best Chaplins, there is a decent narrative framework here to provide snug niches for the jokes. With more drama and fewer gags, Chaplin was compelled to be highly selective about the humor he

used. The result is an almost un-
broken series of ingenious (and appropriate) gags. At mealtime on the
swaying ship, Chaplin and another
passenger "share" a dish because it
slides back and forth between them.
Afterwards Charlie the gamesman
rolls dice and shuffles a deck of
cards like a Mississippi riverboat
gambler gone wild. The sequence in
the restaurant is a triumphant display of theme and variations: Chaplin spots a coin on the floor and
spends five minutes trying to overcome the exquisitely timed obsta-
cles that prevent him from picking it
up. On the other hand, the ironic
contrast between the Statue of Lib-

*THE IMMIGRANT (1917). Charlie and the other immigrants see the
Statue of Liberty.*

THE ADVENTURER (1917). With Edna Purviance

erty and the treatment the immigrants receive from the American sailors, although effective, has received more than its share of praise. It is graced with no particular power or perception and should not be ranked above the comic episodes or even the sly touches Chaplin introduces here and there—for example, the phantom punch that the burly waiter throws at a beaded curtain after demolishing a customer who "was ten cents short."

With *The Adventurer,* Chaplin's last film for Mutual, the pendulum swung back again to slapstick. Devoid of sensibility or naturalism, *The Adventurer* takes up the "mistaken identity" ploy where Chaplin had left it with *The Count.* This time he is an escaped convict who rescues some ladies of leisure from drowning and is welcomed into their set. One of them (Edna Purviance) has a suitor (Eric Campbell) who is displeased, but Charlie's charmingly absurd gallantry at Edna's party the next day goes over well with her. Unfortunately, the imposture ends abruptly when the police arrive to reclaim Charlie. A chase results in temporary capture—and then another escape.

Although *The Adventurer* is no advance over the other Mutuals, it is no regression either. Chaplin's sureness of touch can be felt in the agility and timing of his escape, as he darts Nijinsky-like, over and through the limbs of his would-be captors; the delightful sleight of hand he exhibits in snatching drink after drink at the party; the resourcefulness he summons up in quickly revising a police photo of him in the newspaper to look like the suitor.

By the time Chaplin left Mutual in 1916, his gifts as a comedian were almost inseparable from the growth of his screen persona, the Tramp, and both were nearing perfection. In their final form, the Tramp's comic features were his quirky mannerisms (lifting his hat straight up, turning corners on one foot, hooking his cane in peculiar places); the uniquely Chaplinesque fusion of howling social gaffes and pretenses of elegance (dropping his gloves—and his *cigar*—into his top hat); the effortless displays of physical grace (snatching things out from under people's noses, eluding pursuers in the most confined quarters); the fiendish cunning in his approach to seemingly insurmountable problems (disguising himself as a lamp to throw pursuers off the track); and, of course, the preposterous contradictions in his appearance (oversize shoes, an ill-fitting coat with baggy trousers, and so on). The serious dimensions of the Tramp were his quixotic fixations on beautiful girls; the seediness and disorder of his normal living conditions; his sense of the romantic and lyrical possibilities of life; the compassion, empathy and self-sacrifice of which he was capable. These varied aspects of the Tramp were all there, raw and inchoate, in the Keystone and Essanay comedies, but in his journeyman phase at Mutual he joined them seamlessly. And when he left for First National, he stood at the very brink of greatness.

A tramp is sleeping next to a fence in a vacant lot, with his dog Scraps beside him in a nearby ashcan. Sensing a draft, he looks up, detects a hole in the fence and quickly solves his insulation problem with a dirty handkerchief. Thus begins Chaplin's initial film for First National, *A Dog's Life* (1918), and one of the minor masterpieces of silent-screen comedy. This brilliant amalgam of social satire, down-and-out misery and slapstick comedy conclusively erased any doubts that Chaplin was an artist.

Waking up, the Tramp tries to steal some frankfurters for himself and Scraps, but is detected by a policeman. Eluding capture by means of extreme physical dexterity, he tries to find work at an employment office but is rudely shouldered aside by other applicants. Afterward, stopping at a local tavern, he meets and is taken with a sweet, naïve young singer (Edna Purviance) who has just started working there, but he is hurled into the street when his lack of funds is discovered. Meanwhile, a couple of crooks lift a drunk's wallet, but then lose it to Scraps. Passed along to Charlie, this largesse allows him to reenter the bar in style. The crooks reclaim the wallet by force, but Charlie, knocking one of them unconscious from behind a curtain as they sit talking, extends his hands onto the table as if they were the crook's and gestures expressively. Fooled, the other thief surrenders the wallet, and Charlie and Edna are on their way to a new life on a picturesque farm.

Chaplin's own appraisal of *A Dog's Life* is as apt as any critic's: "I was beginning to think of comedy in a structural sense, and to become conscious of its architectural form. Each sequence implied the next sequence, all of them relating to the whole." In this case, the basic blueprint was a parallel between the lives of the Tramp and the dog Scraps. Profoundly simple but profoundly effective are such implied comparisons as the "beds" each must make do with, their acquisition of food, the injustice and ill treatment they receive from their peers, their theft of the wallet from the original thieves. As in *Easy Street*, the film's social consciousness is not really deep or penetrating, but the new ambiance it affords Chaplin is far more compelling than the relatively denatured settings of films like *The Cure* or *The Adventurer*. Also, the use of satire, though it is unremarkable in its perceptions, widens the range of Chaplin's comedy. Both the satire and the more typically Chaplinesque humor show Chaplin's powers nearing their peak. The Tramp's

A DOG'S LIFE (1918). Charlie and Scraps.

gymnastic adroitness in evading the cop, the split-second timing of the rush to the windows in the employment office, the "puppeteering" sequence with the two crooks—these are routines that no other comedian in 1918 could have conceived, let alone executed.

Chaplin had drawn considerable criticism for his civilian status during World War I, though he made an attempt to enlist and was turned down because of his small stature. He tried to compensate for the deficiencies of his physique by working for the Liberty Bond Drive, which took him to dozens of cities and raised millions for the Allied cause. His greatest gift to the troops, however, was *Shoulder Arms* (1918), his second film for First National.

Civilian audiences were also convulsed by Charlie's progress from ineptitude to military glory and back again. After a poor showing in boot camp, he is sent to France, where he faces the drabness and monotony of trench warfare: sentry duty, waiting for mail, sharing a bottle with equally bored comrades, sniping at Germans. At last an offensive is launched and Charlie captures a number of German soldiers with as little assistance as Sergeant York. Later he is dispatched to spy on the enemy disguised as a tree. Detected, he hides in a half-demolished farmhouse and is com-forted by the owner, a young French girl (Edna Purviance). When she is seized by the Germans, Charlie comes to her rescue. Masquerading as an enemy officer, he not only saves a comrade (Sydney Chaplin) but captures the Kaiser and delivers him to the Allies. In his hour of triumph, however, he awakens in boot camp: it was all a dream.

Discounting a few weak jokes at the beginning, the comic riches of this film emerge from a bottomless purse. The flow of gags in the trench scenes includes Charlie holding aloft a bottle that is accomodatingly opened by enemy fire, putting on a gas mask to eat a package of cheese from home, and obediently crawling into his waterlogged bed, where he breathes through an old phonograph speaker. There is particular joy in the sequence in which Charlie, having come up empty-handed at mail call, pokes his head surreptitiously over someone's shoulder and reads along. The eye movements and facial expressions of Charlie and the other soldier are as expertly synchronized as two sets of electronic scanners. It is a thumbnail sketch of truly desperate vicariousness.

The pinnacle of *Shoulder Arms* is Chaplin's arboreal espionage, justly one of the most renowned comic turns in movie history. Perhaps only God can make a tree, but only

A DOG'S LIFE (1918). Charlie, Edna Purviance, and Scraps are thrown out of a cabaret.

Chaplin could create this camouflaged creature, complete with leaves and bark, who relaxes when the Germans look away, snaps his "branches" back up into place the moment they look back, and frantically avoids being chopped down for firewood by covertly knocking out enemy soldiers one by one.

Structurally, the film is further evidence of Chaplin's growth. The narrative proceeds with logical design from the ordinary to the unusual to the fantastic. The gags are well integrated and grow naturally out of situations that, at least in the first half of the film, have a certain verisimilitude. Indeed, much of what the troops seem to have enjoyed about *Shoulder Arms* was its comparatively realistic detail (e.g., flooded bunkers, military rigidity, hasty, improvised meals). The film's pathos is as smoothly interpolated as its humor. One lovely, beautifully composed shot shows the French girl seated in front of her bombed-out house, with the simple title, "Poor France."

Chaplin followed *Shoulder Arms* with *Sunnyside* (1919). A three-reeler, it may have been inspired by the comedian's friendship with Nijinsky, whom he met in Hollywood in 1917 when the great Russian dancer visited his studio, dubbing his work "balletique."*

The plot is reasonably sound.

*This recalls W.C. Fields' comment on Chaplin after watching one of his films: "He's a goddamn ballet dancer!"

Chaplin plays an overworked factotum with a curious dual job: he divides his time between a hotel and a nearby farm, both owned by the same tyrannical boss. During the early portions of the film we see Charlie's hapless efforts to keep up with his overwhelming duties. His only solace is his romantic fixation on a local farmer's daughter (Edna Purviance) whose attitude toward him is one of gentle tolerance. Herding his employer's cattle home one day, Charlie loses control of them and after some misadventures

At a Liberty Bond rally in April 1918. On the podium with Chaplin: Marie Dressler, Douglas Fairbanks, and Mary Pickford

SHOULDER ARMS (1918). Doughboy Charlie

in the local church, he is knocked unconscious by one of his bovine charges. In a dream sequence, he imagines himself playing Pan to a lovely group of wood nymphs in Grecian costumes, dancing lithely through idyllic surroundings. Awakening, Charlie finds himself back in the cycle of frustration and abuse. The arrival of a city slicker, who begins courting Edna, adds to Charlie's misery. In another dream sequence, he attempts with comical effect to imitate the city man. But, with the latter's departure, Charlie's route to happiness with Edna seems fairly clear.

Seen today, *Sunnyside* looks better than it did to audiences in 1919, who were not very pleased with it. Chaplin taps a congenial flow of comedy from Charlie's twenty-hour-a-day schedule (to save time, he arises fully dressed), his labor-saving devices (obediently, a hen lays eggs for him directly over a frying pan), his problems with animals (he has to coax a cow out of church) and his ludicrous efforts at aping the dapper city man (he converts a pair of socks into spats). In a more dreamy, lyrical vein is the gentle ballet with the nymphs—the centerpiece of the film—which combines serious choreography, comic mishaps and satirical touches aimed at the world of classical dance.

Chaplin's next venture, *A Day's Pleasure* (also 1919), found as little favor with the public as *Sunnyside*. In this one he banished all serious elements in preference for undiluted comedy, mostly slapstick, about a holiday outing that Charlie takes with his family. After problems with their flivver and a quarrel with a policeman, the family boards an excursion boat. There Charlie's problems include seasickness (induced by the rocking of the boat), a deck chair that refuses to unfold properly, and a fistfight with a beefy gentleman who finds Charlie in his wife's lap.

The humor of frustration, rather than ingenious solutions, dominates the film: a car that stops and starts erratically, a minor crisis in which hot tar envelops Charlie and a policeman, the uncooperative deck chair. *A Day's Pleasure* also has its share of tastelessness—Charlie boards the ship by using the outstretched form of a heavy, unattractive woman as a gangplank.

Neither Chaplin nor First National was happy with the reception accorded these two films and Chaplin began casting about for a major project that would equal the genius of *Shoulder Arms*. Seeing the child actor Jackie Coogan in a vaudeville act, Chaplin almost instantly conceived the idea for what was to become *The Kid*: a slum dweller and the orphan he raises. Feeling that this conception might evolve into his masterpiece, Chaplin invested

SHOULDER ARMS (1918). In the trenches

SUNNYSIDE (1919). Charlie with the wood nymphs of his dream

$300,000 and the better part of a year in it. Ever the perfectionist, he is known to have spent a week on scenes that last no more than a minute or two on screen. The Mildred Harris divorce suit obstructed the film's release for a while and Chaplin even had to flee to Utah with his negative in a suitcase to avoid having the film impounded as common property. Once the path was clear, however, he demanded $600,000 from First National, plus a percentage of the gross. The film was released in February, 1921 to almost unanimous praise and a $2,500,000 box office.

The story opens on a young woman (Edna Purviance) leaving a charity hospital with her fatherless infant. Grief-stricken, she abandons it in a rich man's automobile. The baby is eventually rescued from a garbage-littered alley by the Tramp, who raises the boy in his garret. The two live and work together happily—evading the police and the bullies—until representatives of the county orphan asylum show up to claim the Kid. Charlie and he succeed in fleeing from these heartless bureaucrats. Meanwhile Edna has become a famous actress but returns to the slums to do charity work. From an old note she learns that the Kid is her child and

71

A DAY'S PLEASURE (1919). Charlie gets into a fight on an excursion boat.

notifies the authorities. Later the Kid is taken away from Charlie in a flophouse and returned to Edna. The distraught Charlie searches everywhere, then dreams he is in heaven with the Kid. All is beatific—even the neighborhood bully is nice—until some devils sneak in. They encourage the bully's flirtatious wife to "vamp" Charlie, arousing the bully's jealousy. Chaplin takes flight, but he is shot down by the policeman.

Awakened by the real cop, however, the Tramp is led to the actress' home and reunited with his "son."

For many filmgoers in 1921, *The Kid* eclipsed *Shoulder Arms* because it was "more than just a comedy," and it has remained one of Chaplin's best-loved films. At the same time, tolerance for the Edna Purviance subplot has eroded steadily over the years and by 1972 one critic, Gary Carey, described it as "dripping off the screen with mawkishness." He neglected to add, however, that the serious passages in the main narrative trickle down almost as egregiously. If their mawkishness is slightly more bearable, it is because they are played with greater conviction and because of our awareness of their autobiographical roots. For example, Chaplin obviously lavished considerable attention on the cruel attempts by the authorities to separate Charlie and the Kid. Chaplin's own waiflike youth accounts for the unassailable sincerity of this sequence and for the clever bifurcation that critics have noted in his self-portrait: his childhood walks hand in hand with his adult self. But Chaplin has found no way to distinguish this unabashed tear-jerking from its well-known Victorian models.

The redeeming features of *The Kid*, which make it well worth viewing today, are the evidence it provides that Chaplin's ability to integrate humor and narrative was continuing to develop and, of course, the jokes themselves. Charlie's first thwarted attempts to rid himself of the baby, the disarming partnership whereby the Kid breaks windows and Charlie repairs them, Charlie's casual conversion of a ripped blanket into a lounging robe (a virtually archetypal instance of the interplay of elegance and shabbiness in the Tramp's lifestyle), the mock prize-fight atmosphere of the Kid's battle with a neighboring child, the sheer poetry of movement in the efforts of the Tramp and the Kid to conceal the child's presence in the flophouse—these moments all glow with Chaplin's unique comic genius. And they are all the more gratifying for being components in a perfectly organic whole.

The Kid is also distinguished by the wonderful command of fantasy revealed in the dream sequence. Chaplin reports that Sir James Barrie, though praising the film as a whole, deemed this episode irrelevant. Indeed, the only justification for it is its intrinsic drollery and charm. The transition from reality to dream is effortless, as flowers and fairy-tale trimmings appear about the Tramp's slumbering form. The alchemy by which earthly characters and situations find heavenly equivalents is both deft and entertaining (for, in reality, Charlie's nemeses are a policeman, a bully, and a woman). On a deeper level, the last shot of Charlie, a fallen angel with wings beautifully askew, has a forlorn, almost tragic poetry to it that eludes Chaplin when he courts it directly elsewhere in the film.

The relative artistic letdown that afflicted Chaplin's work after *Shoulder Arms* appeared again after *The Kid*. It is not simply that *The*

THE KID (1921). Charlie and the Kid (Jackie Coogan)

Idle Class, released in the fall of 1921, shows Chaplin opting for the diminished emotional and financial demands of a two-reeler; the film is not even close to the level of his best short comedies. Perhaps he was rushing his eight-picture First National contract to completion as soon as possible.

The story and subject matter both had wonderful possibilities. Chaplin plays a dual role—the Tramp and a rather effete member of the leisure class. The wife of the latter (Edna Purviance) comes to join her husband at a fashionable resort community, arriving on the same train as Charlie, who climbs out of the tool compartment under the train. Infuriated that her alcoholic, absentminded husband failed to meet her at the station, Edna takes separate rooms at the hotel where he is staying. Later, on the golf links, Charlie sees her ride by on horseback, and dreams of rescuing her from a runaway steed. Unjustly suspected of picking a pocket, he takes refuge at Edna's masked ball, where she mistakes him for her husband. The real husband, encased in a suit of armor, is infuriated to see Charlie and Edna fondling one another. A fight results, Edna's burly father (Mack Swain) gets into the act and ultimately Charlie has to free his twin from the armor with a can opener. He is ejected from the party and responds to the father's efforts at reconciliation with a kick in the pants.

The film's plot is reminiscent of *The Count* without the polish Chaplin had acquired since 1916. It starts well—a series of grand arrivals at the train station, capped by Charlie rolling anticlimactically out of the tool box. From this point on, the jokes are exceedingly broad. (For example, the self-absorbed rich man strolls nonchalantly out of his room in his underwear.) Inspiration flickers briefly when the dissolute husband, his shoulders apparently shaking in grief over his wife's rebuff, turns to reveal a martini shaker he is working vigorously. Even here, though, Chaplin's timing, which almost never falters, is too slow and he gives the gag away. More important, the opportunity to portray a type completely antithetical to the Tramp is allowed to collapse into low-comedy pranks that are indistinguishable from those associated with the famous "little fellow."

Artistically, Chaplin climbed a short distance above *The Idle Class* with his next film, *Pay Day*, another minor two-reeler. In spite of its largely lower-middle-class milieu, it shouldn't be mistaken for a work of social awareness. Nor does it reveal any of Chaplin's recently cultivated expertise in plotting. Instead, it trails along with drab sequentiality as Charlie, a construc-

THE KID (1921). With Nellie Bly Baker

tion worker, arrives at his job (late, of course), performs his duties with varying degrees of competence, collects his pay, gets drunk with the boys, rides home on a trolley and, echoing *One A.M.*, goes to sleep in the bathtub.

There is a certain up-to-date patina of realism to the story, but actually it is quite atavistic; structurally and thematically, it looks back to the comedies of Chaplin's Essanay and Keystone periods. Furthermore, the warmth and compassion that gave *A Dog's Life* its special luminosity is completely missing. Yet despite these qualifications, *Pay Day* is an agreeable comedy reflecting some of the mature Chaplin's remarkable cleverness. Especially adroit is the trolley sequence, in which Charlie bulls his way onto a crowded car and then gets slowly forced through it and out the other end by the furious ingress of passengers.

Chaplin still owed First National two films, but he persuaded the company to accept *The Pilgrim*, a four-reeler, as payment in full. Although it was twice as good—and as profitable—as most of the non-Chaplin comedies of 1923, it is now a little more famous than it deserves to be. A variation on *The Adventurer*, the story concerns Charlie's exploits after escaping from prison and stealing a minister's clothes. In a small town out West, he is mistaken for the new preacher scheduled to arrive that day, and manages to fake his way through a church service. Later he relaxes in the home of Mrs. Brown and her daughter (Edna Purviance), though the devilishness of a neighborhood child sorely tries his patience. Then an old confederate from his criminal days arrives to complicate matters. Despite Charlie's warnings, he makes off with the Browns' life savings. In a dramatic episode in the town saloon, Charlie retrieves the money and returns it to Edna. In the meantime, his ruse has been discovered and the local sheriff arrests him. But honesty has its rewards. Leading Charlie back to jail, the sheriff decides to turn him loose at the Mexican border.

Its reputation notwithstanding, *The Pilgrim* is a highly uneven work, showing signs of haste and indifference. Most of the humor is keyed to the sharp, presumably funny, contrast between Charlie the convict and Charlie the minister. Unfortunately, the expository material at the beginning is so severely telescoped that we never have a sense of Charlie's criminal nature. Even *The Pilgrim*'s most celebrated scene, the sermon in which Charlie pantomimes the story of David and Goliath, seems unremarkable. The stark antithesis inherent in the famous tale makes the miming seem comparatively facile.

In spite of these flaws, *The Pil-*

THE KID (1921). Charlie and the Kid elude the police.

THE IDLE CLASS (1921). With Eric Campbell

grim does have its pleasures. The small-town atmosphere is well evoked. Charlie's reversions to highly unecclesiastical behavior are frequently funny, as in the church service, where he converts his sermon into a vaudeville performance, bounding off stage and then returning for his bows. The later scene with the obnoxious child, in which Charlie manfully smiles through a series of playful torments, has a nice Fieldsian quality that wipes away some of the treacle left behind by *The Kid*—especially when Char-lie, at last unobserved by other adults, kicks the brat across the room. Also entertaining is the stately march of the tall, self-important deacon and his tiny new "minister" to and from church; it represents one of Chaplin's few attempts at comedy of manners. In this connection, it is worth noting that the bluenoses of Pennsylvania paid this film the ultimate compliment of banning it for irreverence: just the quality Chaplin was striving for.

Liberated from First National

PAY DAY (1922). Charlie attempts to hide from his wife in the bathtub.

THE PILGRIM (1923). Phony clergyman Charlie and a suspicious cop

THE PILGRIM (1923). The "pilgrim" delivers a sermon.

after three years, Chaplin startled
his new colleagues at United Artists
by announcing that his first film for
UA would be a serious drama and
that his own role in it would be no
more than a walk-on. The germ of
the story was supplied by Peggy
Hopkins Joyce, a much-married
society butterfly and sometime actress. She kept Chaplin enthralled
with spicy anecdotes of her life in
France. Fleshed out by Chaplin,

these became *A Woman of Paris*,
the tale of an artist, a kept woman
and a debonair playboy, set against
the backdrop of the Parisian demi-
monde.

The story centers on Jean and
Marie (Carl Miller and Edna Purviance), young lovers in a small
French town who plan to run away
to Paris to escape the harassment of
their parents. The sudden death of
Jean's father and an ill-timed tele-

A WOMAN OF PARIS (1923). With Carl Miller and Edna Purviance

A WOMAN OF PARIS (1923). A scene showing Chaplin's sense of time and place

phone call leads Marie to believe she has been abandoned by Jean, and she goes to Paris on her own. There she becomes the jaded, discontented mistress of Pierre (Adolphe Menjou), an affluent man-about-town. She is happy when, by chance, she encounters Jean, who has come to Paris with his mother (Lydia Knott) to make his way as a painter. Though disturbed by her illicit status, Jean is still in love with her and proposes marriage. She is tempted to accept—if only to arouse Pierre's jealousy —but rebuffs Jean when she overhears him quarreling with his mother about her. The tragic denouement comes at a nightclub where Jean, after a violent altercation with Pierre, shoots himself. Miserable and contrite, Marie is ul-

*A WOMAN OF PARIS (1923). With Carl Miller, Edna Purviance, and
Adolphe Menjou*

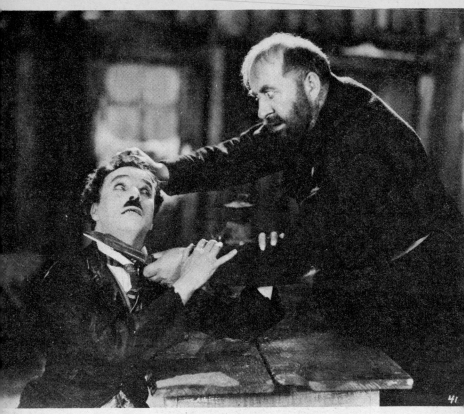

THE GOLD RUSH (1925). With Mack Swain

timately reconciled with Jean's mother and the two women return to the country, to devote themselves to the care of orphans.

A Woman of Paris, released in 1923, was received with enthusiasm by the critics but snubbed by the public, which missed the rigidly predictable story lines and broad gestures of Griffith, DeMille and other filmmakers of the day. In-

deed, the depth and subtlety of the film soon made it a landmark, despite its poor showing at the box office. Intended to launch Edna Purviance on an independent career, it made Adolphe Menjou a star instead (in the type of role he was to play for most of his career) and simultaneously inaugurated a long series of imitations—Harry d'Abbadie d'Arrast's significantly titled *A Gentleman of Paris*, Monta Bell's *Broadway After Dark*, Ernst Lubitsch's *The Marriage Circle*, and his other cosmopolitan comedies.

The movie is highly eclectic, blending a number of different styles and modes. The least healthy influence is that of Thomas Hardy, whose spirit can be felt in the two excruciating coincidences that begin this "drama of fate." Objections might also be raised to the sermonlike tone of the last scene, in which rural goodness is contrasted to townly decadence in a way that owes more to nineteenth-century

THE GOLD RUSH (1925). Charlie and villainous Tom Murray

morality than to real life.

Despite some initial implausibilities and the preachy tone of the last scene, *A Woman of Paris* is a mature and subtle work. The events of the story develop quite logically, dictated by character and social situation, not theatricality and didacticism. For example, Marie's repentence at the end is inspired by the tragedy she has caused, not by any remorse over her "lost virtue." Indeed, throughout most of the film Marie's outstanding characteristic is her shallowness, her addiction to the material and superficial gaiety of *la vie Parisienne*, as embodied by Pierre. We are in no doubt that she is drawn to her old sweetheart, to the prospect he holds out of home and family, but the pull is not strong enough to snap her ties with Pierre. Hence, her rejection of Jean is the film's triumph of character over contrivance, motivation over manipulation: Chaplin makes it clear that the overheard remark is *not* another blow of fate but rather the comfortable excuse Marie needs to go back to Pierre. This precipitates the confrontation and suicide. With her inescapable blandness, Edna Purviance was well suited to play a comparatively empty, frivolous woman from whom only catastrophe can call forth some real grief and penitence.

Similarly, Carl Miller's Jean comes across as a person rather than a personification. He is capable of innocent, untroubled affection; deeply conflicted love; romantic anguish; shame, humiliation and self-destruction. His attachment to his mother—with its obvious autobiographical significance for Chaplin—is so understated as to actually seem the normal and human thing it is, rather than a maudlin lunge at the audience's heartstrings.

Nominally the hero, Jean is displaced by Pierre, one of the few credible villains in silent films. Gay, witty, self-assured, but with an impeccable sense of form, Pierre typifies the Parisian boulevardier, a man of glittering surfaces and no depths at all.

In creating these portraits, Chaplin keeps the acting scaled down to human dimensions at all times, though he leaves no doubt of the powerful emotions beating below the surface. After Marie's departure following the reunion scene, a single look of misery, tinged with anger, on Jean's face conveys his feelings about her harlotry. Particularly brilliant is the dispute between Marie and Pierre over the pleasures of domesticity. Pierre's ironic view is neatly symbolized for him by a mother and her squalling kids outside on the street. Angrily, Marie throws her pearls out the window to rebut Pierre and his whole way of life. But then her basic dishonesty is

THE GOLD RUSH (1925). With Georgia Hale

revealed when she runs frantically to retrieve them from a passing derelict who has picked them up. Carving an extra stroke into the brilliance, Chaplin has her turn around and give the man a reward, salving her conscience and acting out the role of the great lady at the same time.

Had he continued in the direction of *A Woman of Paris*, Chaplin might have made a significant contribution to serious filmmaking. But at this stage in his career he craved the blend of aesthetic qualities that would bring him popular as well as critical success. Since his next film was one of the principal glories of screen comedy, it is difficult to complain too much.

The Gold Rush, considered by many Chaplin's greatest film, is also the one he has said he would like to be remembered for. The achievement did not come easily. As it was impossible to shoot in the Klondike, the actual setting of the film, Chaplin had to construct a replica of Alaska's Chilkoot Pass in the Rocky Mountains of Nevada. Working at a height of 10,000 feet, Chaplin's crew built a pathway 2,300 feet long at a cost of over $30,000. Overall production costs were about $600,000 and fourteen months went into the film before it was finished. Released in August 1925, the picture was an immediate success, adding $2,000,000 to Chaplin's rapidly swelling private fortune.

The inspiration for the film was the Donner Party, a group of pioneers who were stranded in the Rockies in 1847 and were driven to cannibalism. That Chaplin was able to convert their grim experiences to comedy is a tribute to his genius. His story, worked up with the technical assistance of an actual hobo, begins in the Chilkoot Pass, where Charlie, a lone prospector, is struggling through the snow. During a storm he seeks refuge in the cabin of Black Larson, a notorious Alaskan outlaw and is soon joined there by another prospector, Big Jim (Mack Swain). Larson leaves to find help but does not return. Near starvation, Charlie and Jim boil one of Charlie's shoes and eat it for dinner. Subsequently, a providential bear provides them with a real meal and Jim sets out to find his claim. There he encounters Larson, who fells him with a blow from a shovel, inducing amnesia.

Meanwhile, Charlie wanders into a Klondike town, where, in the saloon, he immediately falls in love with the tempestuous dance-hall girl, Georgia (Georgia Hale). When two prospectors leave the Tramp in charge of their cabin, as they head off in search of gold, Charlie invites Georgia and some of the other dance hall girls to dinner on New

THE CIRCUS (1928). With Merna Kennedy

Year's Eve and they accept, but only in jest. The Tramp is left to "celebrate" alone over a resplendent table he has prepared. When Georgia discovers what has happened, she is remorseful. Later Big Jim stumbles into town, unable to recall the location of his spectacular claim. However, reunited with Charlie, who can lead him back to the original cabin, he is exultant and promises his friend a 50-50 split. Back at the cabin, another storm breaks loose and when Jim and Charlie awake, the cabin is dangling over a cliff.* Despite the cabin's teetering back and forth, the two avoid plunging into the abyss. In the last scene, they are multimillionaires about to sail for home. By coincidence, Georgia is leaving also and she soon becomes Charlie's fiancée.

The technical side of *The Gold Rush* (especially the lighting and editing) can be faulted, but the rest of it is—like Big Jim's strike—a mountain of gold. As always in Chaplin's work, most of the humor is generated by the Tramp's struggle against adversity, which often

takes amusing forms, and his imaginative strategies for overcoming it. Here the scope of his conflict, usually limited to society, is widened to include nature. Thus, in the movie's most famous sequence, Charlie wins a round in his elemental battle against starvation by eating his shoe, while pretending it is an epicurean delight.

The other well-known set piece in *The Gold Rush* is the "Oceana Roll," in which Charlie, dreaming of the entertainment he will offer the dance-hall girls, spears two bread rolls with a couple of forks and makes them simulate a pair of dancing feet. The tour de force is enhanced when the camera isolates the Tramp against a black background. The result is that—as he makes the rolls dance, scamper offstage, return for a curtain call—they appear to be *his* feet, part of a distorted, misshapen figure glimpsed in a fun-house mirror. His hopes of pleasing the girls through these miniature music hall turns (the best he has to offer, since he can't dance himself) are among Chaplin's most lyrical effects.

Indeed, Charlie's desire to please is one of the major motivations in the film. Smiling servilely, he apes Big Jim's words and gestures in an angry dialogue with Black Larson. Later he compliantly hands over the more "succulent" portion of the shoe. The main burden of the film's

*Donald McCaffrey (*Focus on Chaplin*, Prentice-Hall, 1971) calls attention to this episode as the most cinematic sequence in *The Gold Rush*: "The medium takes over: editing, contrasting shots, titles and special effects help create the comic horror that has been thrust upon the two men." But of course the mating of comedy and thrills must be credited to Harold Lloyd, not Chaplin.

THE CIRCUS (1928). With Allan Garcia

pathos, however, is carried by poignant episodes concerning Georgia, whose attitude toward Charlie passes through surprisingly well-defined stages on its progress from indifference to love.

The Gold Rush is probably Chaplin's most successful union of comedy and sadness. Georgia's discovery of her picture, lovingly hidden under the tramp's pillow, is quickly followed by the hotfoot Charlie receives from one of the other girls; the awkward invitation he extends is offset by the subsequent explosion of joy he directs at the pillows, filling the room with billowing feathers (a nice correlative to the swirls of snow outside); the poignancy of the empty dinner table is soon relieved by the charm of the dancing rolls.

Topping *The Gold Rush* would have been an impossibility, but trying to imitate it would have been a mistake. Chaplin wisely chose a new setting and a more modest story. Given his addiction to brokenhearted clowns, it was inevitable that sooner or later he should produce his own *Pagliacci*. Deciding on a circus setting, he indulged the same expensive taste for realism he had cultivated in *The Gold Rush*, constructing his own big top, complete with all the trimmings. The production costs on the new film, titled *The Circus*, amounted to nearly $1,000,000. It

was largely finished by December 1926, but the final editing and release was delayed until early in 1928 by the Lita Grey divorce action (a ghastly replay of Chaplin's experience with *The Kid*).

In *The Circus*, Chaplin's clown was, of course, the now-familiar Tramp. Chased by the police, who wrongly suspect him of a robbery, the Tramp hides in various sideshow exhibitions at the circus. (So does the real crook, who is using Charlie as a decoy.) Finally the Tramp is pursued straight into the big top. There he creates havoc, entertaining the spectators far more exhilaratingly than the trained clowns. Impressed by the Tramp's performance, the owner of the circus (Allan Garcia) hires him as a performer. Charlie immediately makes friends with the owner's daughter (Merna Kennedy), a bareback rider who is badly mistreated by her father. Though the Tramp's love grows, the girl gives her heart to Rex (Harry Crocker), a handsome trapeze artist. When Rex fails to show up one day, Charlie goes on in his place, hoping to supplant him with the girl as well. He survives the high-wire ordeal triumphantly, but is fired afterwards when he tries to stop the boss from abusing his daughter. She attempts to run away with Charlie, but in a burst of self-sacrifice, he promotes her marriage to Rex in-

THE CIRCUS (1928). With Henry Bergman

stead. The couple is reconciled with the owner and rejoins the circus, as the Tramp heads off down the road in the opposite direction.

The Circus is generally regarded as a minor film of Chaplin's major period, a sensible assessment. The first ten minutes, however, are as good as anything the comedian ever did. After a brief introductory sequence under the big top succinctly establishes the circus ambiance, the

CITY LIGHTS (1931). With his drunken millionaire friend, Harry Myers

camera "discovers" Charlie hanging around the sideshows and the fun begins: the Tramp stealing bites from a baby's hot dog, while its father's back is turned; the Tramp grandiosely ordering his own hot dogs when a wallet mysteriously falls into his hands; the surprised expression he and the thief exchange when they find each other fleeing the police side by side; the hilarious confusion when Charlie is stalked in the house of mirrors, where his policeman-antagonist lunges impotently at one reflection after another. Then Chaplin transcends even this superbly executed material, when the Tramp and the thief, still trying to avoid the watchful eyes of the police, pretend they are mechanical, Swiss-clock figures, marching in various directions. Borrowed by Sid Caesar, this routine later became the famous television sketch, "The Clock."

Charlie's disruptions of the circus

performance have the same freshness and élan. From this point on, however, the flame of Chaplin's inspiration burns fitfully, flickering quite low when the Tramp auditions for the ringmaster. The premise seems to be that he is comically inept in his conscious efforts at being funny. But Chaplin does not put sufficient aesthetic distance between the moth-eaten slapstick he is trying to ridicule and the Tramp's own performance. A later scene in which Charlie is inadvertently trapped in the lion's cage is amusing, but the comic finale on the high wire—with Charlie tottering every which way, plagued by monkeys, and other distractions—is only adequate. It is all too clearly another cliff-hanger in the Harold Lloyd manner. It is not as good as Lloyd's own work and neither is it as good as the typically Chaplinesque quality of the initial episodes.

Similarly Chaplinesque is the Tramp's bittersweet relationship with the bareback rider, which appears to reflect Chaplin's glumness over his marital problems, at least indirectly. The mood that is generated by this element of the film is one of intense, almost embarrassing masochism and self-pity. When the girl offers to run away with him, the Tramp nobly restores her to the Man She Really Loves. Compounding his self-abnegation, the Tramp serves as the witness at their wedding and exuberantly pelts the couple with rice. Perhaps this masochistic outpouring was as close as Chaplin could come to expressing his deep sense of persecution at the hands of women.

Far more credible and psychologically intriguing is the unusual scene in which Charlie's "spirit" rises angrily out of his body to demolish Rex. The doppelgänger then completes the job by kicking dirt over his rival's inert form, as if to wholly erase his existence. The savagery of the Tramp's feelings —the worm turning—takes the audience far deeper into the human psyche than most of Chaplin's overt attempts at depth psychology.

Fundamentally, then, The Circus is as good as the best of Chaplin's routines in it and as bad as the worst. But when the routines are bad, they're never really awful and when they're good, they're wonderful in the unique way of the greatest film comedy.

The transition from silent films to talkies in the late twenties caught Chaplin squarely in the middle of a costly project—City Lights, a film he began in 1928. He had set to work on the movie only a month after The Circus, the dual source of his inspiration being the idea of a poor blind girl and the song "La Violetera," introduced to this country by the Spanish singer Raquel Mueller. When sound films took

CITY LIGHTS (1931). With Virginia Cherrill

CITY LIGHTS (1931). With Hank Mann (in white shorts)

hold, Chaplin halted production, then courageously decided to complete his film.

From the beginning *City Lights* was beset by problems other than the advent of sound. Chaplin's desire for a new Trilby to play his leading lady led him to Virginia Cherrill, a young divorcee with no acting experience, whom he discovered at a boxing match. In the course of filming, she was nearly fired several times. Henry Clive, originally cast as the millionaire, was not so lucky. Chaplin discharged him (for refusing to dive into the studio pool) and then had to reshoot most of his scenes with a new actor, Harry Myers. It was small wonder, then, that production costs topped $1,000,000 and that the film was not released until 1931. "I've spent every penny I possess on *City Lights*," Chaplin told Sam Gold-

99

CITY LIGHTS (1931). Charlie shyly acknowledges his identity to the girl.

wyn. "If it is a failure, I believe it will strike a deeper blow than anything else that has ever happened to me in this life."

The central premise in *City Lights* emerges early on when the Tramp saves the life of a suicidal millionaire (Myers), who thereafter becomes Charlie's intimate friend—but only when he's drunk. In his sober state, he doesn't even recognize Charlie. In another strand of the story, the Tramp himself plays millionaire with a blind flower girl (Cherrill) he has met.

Moved by her predicament, he tries to pry loose $1,000 from his friend for the operation the girl needs to restore her sight. When the man's abrupt alternations in mood make this impossible, Charlie seeks work—first as a street cleaner, then as a boxer. Neither produces the needed cash, but when the Tramp next crosses the millionaire's path, his "friend" is drunk again and he seizes the opportunity to ask for the $1,000. Struck on the head by burglars, the millionaire sobers up once more and Charlie is suddenly viewed as a thief. He flees the police, drops the money off with the girl and is later apprehended and sent to prison. After his release, a chance meeting brings him face to face with the girl, who can now see. She recognizes him from his touch and is moved—but both are a little embarrassed by the Tramp's shabby appearance. The last shot is a close-up of Charlie's nervous grin.

There is probably no one who would deny *City Lights* a place among Chaplin's masterpieces and for many it is the summit of Chaplin's art. These claims can be conceded without ignoring the few weaknesses among the many strengths in this "comedy romance." From his earliest screen appearances, Chaplin had been accused of frequent vulgarities. Even allowing for the corsetted tastes and heavily starched mores of pre-swinging America, there are some objectionable moments in Chaplin's films. In the case of *City Lights*, the film has to answer for such gags as the drunken millionaire pouring liquor down the front of the Tramp's baggy trousers and for some smarmy humor about bodily functions in a locker-room scene.

These deficiencies in *City Lights* comedy are matched on the film's serious plane by the inadequacy of its leading lady. From Edna Purviance to Merna Kennedy, Chaplin's "discoveries" were never more than sufficient unto the day—and unto the limited tasks he assigned them, providing pretty ornamentation. But in *City Lights*, Chaplin broadened his requirements to include a high degree of expressiveness and then filled the part with an amateur who could not meet these demands. Even with Chaplin's extensive coaching, Cherrill could not manage more than a faint grimace of awkwardness on seeing her benefactor at long last. The scene is played with tact and restraint, but it only works half as well as it should because only one of the two participants—Chaplin—projects any emotion. After all, there is an inherent bathos to this story of a blind waif and Chaplin needed all the help he could get to overcome it.

These reservations having been aired, the rest of the film can be praised wholeheartedly. Its joyful array of Chaplin's comic devices ranges from deflations of official pomposity (in the first scene a majestic statue is unveiled to reveal the Tramp sleeping on top of it); to exuberant slapstick (Chaplin using a seltzer bottle to douse a wealthy lady whose dress is accidentally ignited); to highly refined pantomime (savoring a nude statue in an art gallery, the Tramp disguises his lasciviousness with the lofty pose of the connoisseur); to a superbly balletic boxing match (with Charlie pirouetting frantically out of punching range).

These uproarious comic passages, balanced against the serious segments of the film, confer a structural soundness and an almost perfect harmony on *City Lights*. Its pattern of vicissitudes, uncertainty and sudden reversals in the Tramp's life culminate with lovely, surprising consistency in the ambiguous, uncertain ending, as the Tramp smiles at the flower girl with an unforgettable mixture of fear and hope.

On reading accounts of the open-armed joy with which the world embraced this film on its release in February 1931, it is impossible not to exult with Chaplin in his extraordinary personal and professional triumph. Swimming stubbornly against the current, he brought out a silent film in 1931 that pleased nearly everybody and grossed some $5,000,000.

City Lights was the last film Chaplin made which can be regarded as pure art, untouched by didactic intentions. With his next movie, *Modern Times*, a new Chaplin began to appear, still bright and funny and charming but with a steadily darkening brow, unhappy about the course of events in the modern world, anxious to share his thoughts on the subject with his public, to play spokesman and commentator for his age. In *Modern Times*, this rather schoolmasterish Chaplin is specifically concerned with the Depression and the effects of industrialism on mankind. In the course of delivering his lecture, he lifts his famous creation, the Tramp, out of the shadows of the late nineteenth century, his true temporal home, and thrusts him into the overmechanized glare of the twentieth century.

In any event, the plot that Chaplin has spun around this new version of the Tramp is loose and episodic, leaving him plenty of room for his old antics. It begins in a factory where his inability to adapt to conveyor-belt routine has humorous consequences: he cripples the assembly-line rhythm by missing one of the bolts he is supposed to tighten, gets trapped in one of the machines, is victimized by a "feeding machine" and goes berserk with his wrench after a day of turning screws. Later, on another job, he

SOCIAL CRITIC, POLITICAL OBSERVER, PHILOSOPHER

falls off the back of a truck holding a red danger flag and suddenly finds himself leading a Communist demonstration. This earns him a jail term. Released, he meets a gamin (Paulette Goddard) and after helping her escape from the police and the juvenile authorities, he moves in with her in a shack by the waterfront. Next Charlie goes to work as a night watchman in a department store, where he and the girl frolic. Unfortunately, the Tramp is too nice to some burglars who break in and he is soon back in jail. When his term is up, he joins the girl again, who is now working in a cabaret. Hired as a singing waiter, he delights the patrons with a gibberish song knitted together from a half dozen different languages. Before he can enjoy his success, the juvenile officers reappear and he and the gamin must flee. In our last glimpse of them, they are heading down the road.

The social and political content of *Modern Times* has long been controversial, with the left praising its "proletarian virtues" and the right damning it as "Communist propaganda." But, as many observers

MODERN TIMES (1936). With Paulette Goddard

have pointed out, Chaplin's satire seems directed against technology and industrial dehumanization, not capitalism. Certainly the film does not urge its audience onto the barricades. In fact, it advocates no remedies—Marxist or otherwise —for the problems it deals with. Far from aligning itself with any political orthodoxy, the film evades the complex issues it raises, fleeing through the back door into a Rousseauean primitivism, bucolic and footloose. In the end Chaplin's hero and heroine speed away from "modern times" into the past, away from realism and back to the romance of the road.

Another school of thought on *Modern Times*, recognizing the dimness of Chaplin's sociopolitical perceptions, has endeavored to jettison his ideas from the discussion and concentrate on his comedy. By this reasoning the laughs redeem the intellectual vacuity. But, as was the case with *Easy Street* and *A Dog's Life*, it probably makes more sense to view Chaplin's critique of modern society as an extension of the perimeters of his comedy. To be sure, the humor—not the ideas—is what counts, but the particular type of humor could have arisen only from a critique of the sort Chaplin undertakes.

Apart from the debate over the film's intellectual value, there is a general feeling among students of Chaplin that his powers were beginning to ebb with *Modern Times*. But even a casual analysis of the film will show that the old Chaplinesque ingredients are still there, and it is hard to see in what way they are inferior to their earlier versions. The seriocomic Tramp is the same, as is his companion, a pretty street urchin with a background saturated in the squalor and pathos that had such a hold on Chaplin's heart.

In terms of comedy, Charlie's unequal struggle with the gigantic machine he works on is only his old difficulty with objects and equipment, projected here on a magnified scale. In the same way, the mad choreography of his flight from dozens of workers and supervisors in the factory scene has the same agility and rhythm he previously displayed in escaping from policemen. Nor does the pattern require any adjustment for the "perilous comedy" of the department store scene, where Charlie, blindfolded, unknowingly roller skates near a four-story drop. The only novel episode in the film is the introduction of Charlie the song-and-dance man in the cabaret sequence. His multilingual number to the tune of "Titana" is, in addition to being one of the highpoints of the film, the Tramp's one concession to speech and his creator's last eloquent assertion of the universality of his comedy.

MODERN TIMES (1936). Overcome by the machinery, Charlie goes berserk.

Again, one has to marvel at the audacity of a filmmaker who was willing to bring out a movie with practically no spoken dialogue in 1936, eight years into the sound era. To be sure, Chaplin hedged his bets somewhat by using a shooting script for the first time in his career. This allowed him to complete the film in ten months time and at a cost of only $1,500,000, a modest sum considering the sets that were required for the factory scenes. Made of wood and rubber, they simulated steel very convincingly. Nevertheless, Chaplin's risk was enormous and though the film received mixed reviews and the initial returns were disappointing, he was ultimately vindicated: it has since joined earlier Chaplin films in immortality.

Despite some strong dissent on the "profundity" of *Modern Times*, Chaplin felt encouraged to continue as a social and political pundit. During the thirties, he had become active in anti-fascist, anti-Nazi circles and a withering satire on Hitler seemed like the best contribution he could make to the movement. In one of his rare acknowledgments of outside assistance, Chaplin credits Alexander Korda, the British producer, as the originator of the basic device behind his next film *The Great Dictator* (1940): the amazing physical similarity between Chaplin and Hitler.

The plot of *The Great Dictator* is more intricate than previous Chaplin films. It provides the comedian with two roles: Adenoid Hynkel, the dictator of Tomania and an unnamed Jewish barber, who are look-alikes. We are introduced to Hynkel at a rally, where he frantically harangues the crowd, denouncing democracy, free speech and Jews. Afterwards, he turns the storm troopers loose in the ghetto where the barber resists the soldiers and tries to protect Hannah, (Paulette Goddard), a young Jewish girl they are persecuting. Both are saved by the intercession of Schultz (Reginald Gardiner), a minister of Hynkel's whom the barber aided during World War I.

Meanwhile, Hynkel plots the invasion of neighboring Austerlich, a plan which requires him to entertain Benzino Napaloni (Jack Oakie), dictator of Bacteria, who also has designs on Austerlich and who must be persuaded to postpone them. Ultimately, the barber and Schultz (who has lost his government post and joined the Jewish rebels) plot the overthrow of Hynkel but are captured and sent to a concentration camp. Simultaneously, Hannah flees to a farm in Austerlich. Schultz and the barber escape from the camp and, through a complicated series of events, the barber is mistaken for Hynkel. He soon finds himself leading the Tomanian armies into Austerlich. When asked

MODERN TIMES (1936). Charlie and pal Chester Conklin tend the machines.

to address his victorious troops and the conquered Austerlichians, however, he uses it as an opportunity to make an impassioned appeal for peace and brotherhood.

An appreciation of *The Great Dictator* must start prior to the film itself. Quite apart from the quality of the movie, Chaplin must be saluted for having the courage to make it. The issue is not silence versus sound this time, but the boldness that was required to produce such a vehemently anti-Hitler movie in 1940, before our entry in the war, and to portray a heroic Jew, with anti-Semitism at its peak.

Some criticism has been lodged against *The Great Dictator* on the grounds that it is politically naïve and its subject unsuitable for burlesque, but it is more accurately viewed in the same way as *Modern Times:* as an expanded stage for Chaplin's talents. This time, however, his targets were specifically (and topically) political. Moreover, it afforded him the opportunity to take the plunge into talkies in a vehicle comfortably tailored to his abilities. His gift for verbal mimicry, well-known to his friends, was put to use in satirizing Hitler. At the same time, as the barber—a Tramp-like figure—Chaplin was free to remain more or less silent, thus preserving the integrity of his persona until the messianic speech at the end.

Some of the anti-Hitler jokes miss the mark (falling downstairs, for example, was not one of Hitler's peculiarities), but far more of them are deliciously on target. The Nuremburg-style tirade, seething with random ferocities and expressed in a nonsense German clogged with gutturals, is burlesque raised to the highest possible level. The same level is attained again and again by the demonstrations of Hynkel's pomposity and self-involvement: using an elaborate series of subordinates to summon a secretary; rushing to the piano for a few stormy arpeggios; climbing up and down the curtain to the strains of *Lohengrin;* wetting an envelope on the outstretched tongue of an underling. The expressions of megalomania are capped by Hynkel's famous ballet with a large balloon representing the globe, a sequence that deserves all the superlatives that have been heaped on it.

Nor is *The Great Dictator* lacking in traditional Tramp-style humor. The little fellow has a balletic sequence of his own, dancing the length of a street and back on his heels after having been brained accidentally by Hannah. Even more impressive is the celebrated "shaving scene," in which the barber performs his duties in rhythmic synchronization with Brahms' "Hungarian Dance No. 5," a gag that saw

THE GREAT DICTATOR (1940). As Hynkel, Dictator of Tomania

its first rudimentary use in *The Vagabond*.

Some of the characteristic Chaplin elements turn up in less fortunate manifestations. The controlled pathos that gave solidity to *City Lights* becomes lugubrious in *The Great Dictator*. The surging violins that bathe Goddard's scenes are embarrassing, and so is she. In *Modern Times*, where her only task was to exude a wordless vitality, she was quite adequate. Here where she not only has to speak but to "typify the whole Jewish race" (Chaplin's description), she sounds painfully awkward—even allowing for the fact that the lines Chaplin has given her are themselves stumbling and graceless. The rest of the secondary players help make up for Goddard. Perhaps out of insecurity over making a talkie, Chaplin chose, for the first time in his career, to work with seasoned professionals; in addition to Oakie and Gardiner, Billy Gilbert (as Herring) and Henry Daniell (as Garbitsch) were on hand. Of the $2,000,000 Chaplin spent on *The Great Dictator*, not enough seems to have gone into the sets, which have a jerry-built look that is especially crippling in the ghetto scenes and at Hannah's papier-mâché farm in Austerlich. The most universally condemned aspect of the movie is undoubtedly its concluding five-minute oration, a collection of noble platitudes delivered by Chaplin rather than his character: "I should like to help everyone if possible—Jew, Gentile, black man, white," "More than machinery we need humanity," "In the name of democracy, let us unite," etc., etc.

On another level, the film is interesting for its suggestions of schizophrenia in Chaplin. In their book *The Little Fellow*,* Peter Cotes and Thelma Niklaus call attention to the remarkable parallels in birth and origins between Chaplin and Hitler (the similarity in personal appearance is obvious). They further bolster their analogy with a stark quote from one of Chaplin's best friends, Sam Goldwyn: "Chaplin loves power—as no one else whom I have ever seen loves it." The tales of Chaplin's despotic rule over his film productions are legion in Hollywood. Yet he was capable of the gentleness he projected so winningly into the Tramp. Given this dual nature, it is not surprising to learn that two of the roles he most wanted to play were Napoleon and Christ.

It would be wrong to leave the subject of *The Great Dictator* on a negative note, since its many superb comic sequences tip the scales in its favor. Like *Modern Times*, its popularity has grown over

*Peter Cotes and Thelma Niklaus. *The Little Fellow*, (New York: The Citadel Press, 1965),

THE GREAT DICTATOR (1940). With Napaloni (Jack Oakie), Dictator of Bacteria

the years and it is likely to survive as long as interest in the Third Reich does.

His next film *Monsieur Verdoux*, had its origins in a conversation with Orson Welles, who suggested a film built around the French Bluebeard, Landru. Chaplin subsequently bought full rights to the project from Welles and set to work. As Chaplin conceived it, the idea offered him the opportunity for an elaboration and updating of his sociopolitical outlook; a chance for an indirect attack on a society that was, at this juncture in his life, making things very unpleasant for him; and a forum for expressing the misogyny he had built up during three unsuccessful marriages.

Verdoux, the refined and sophisticated boulevardier, though retaining a few hints of the Tramp, was essentially a new departure for Chaplin. The Frenchman makes his living by marrying wealthy old maids and then doing them in for their money. He has just dispatched his latest, Thelma Couvais, when we first meet him. To save his stock market investments, Verdoux is soon compelled to murder another spouse, Lydia, (Margaret Hoffman) after which he returns to his "real" wife, Mona (Mady Correll) an invalid, and his young son, both of whom he loves deeply.

Soon, however, Verdoux is off to yet another wife, the rambunctious Annabella (Martha Raye), who refuses to surrender any of her money to him. Verdoux then adds a devastating new poison to his arsenal and plans to try it out on a girl (Marilyn Nash) he picks up in the street. Unfortunately, she proves too sympathetic and he lets her go. In a later scene he tries to use the poison on Annabella but fails; a subsequent attempt to drown Annabella is also unsuccessful. After a gap of several years—during which time Verdoux has gone bankrupt and lost his wife and child—the story resumes with a chance meeting between the now embittered Verdoux and the girl he decided not to poison. They dine together and Verdoux is spotted by the Couvais family, ever on the lookout for Thelma's murderer. Arrested, Verdoux is swiftly tried, convicted and sentenced to the gallows. Before his demise, however, he wittily and suavely rebuffs a priest's effort to awaken his contrition, insisting that his is a guilt that the entire world shares.

Monsieur Verdoux antagonized the American public and most film reviewers of the time. Chaplin, who anticipated a gross of $12,000,000, found himself with the first failure of his career. However, the film's reputation was kept alive by a more favorable European reception and by James Agee's effusive three-part review in *The Nation*. With the Chaplin revival in the sixties, the

THE GREAT DICTATOR (1940). With Paulette Goddard

THE GREAT DICTATOR (1940). With Robert O. Davis and Reginald Gardiner

situation was reversed dramatically, and the minority view became those—most notably Dwight Macdonald—who *didn't* like the film.

In this "comedy of murders," the villain is not the killer and thief Verdoux, but rather society. Verdoux turns criminal as a result of social injustice (when he is . discharged from his job in the bank after thirty years), and his thefts and homicides are only unadorned reflections of capitalist exploitation and warfare. This awareness of motive elevates Verdoux above the common swarm of bourgeois hypocrites, but Chaplin insists, quite needlessly, on ennobling Verdoux by placing a crippled wife and infant son at the center of his world. Supporting them is the emotionally irresistible excuse for Verdoux's crimes. Lest we miss the point, an overripe romantic theme

115

MONSIEUR VERDOUX (1947). In the title role

MONSIEUR VERDOUX (1947). With Martha Raye

introduces them, the child gurgles lovably, and the camera lingers on the wife's useless legs. Chaplin further stacks the deck by making Verdoux's victims unpleasant or frivolous. They won't be missed.

The film's comedic requirements tend to erode M. Verdoux's premises, however, since Verdoux is made to throw himself into his work with obvious relish. Neither economic necessity nor moral convictions can explain the fusillade of bouquets the merry Verdoux directs at Madame Grosnay, one of his conquests; the cooing blandishments he exchanges with Annabella; the love of his "craft" he reveals in skillfully engineering Lydia's downfall.

The slapstick episodes in *Monsieur Verdoux* are moderately enjoyable, but they also violate what is supposed to be a sardonic Shavian mood and separate Chaplin from the character he is playing. Is Ver-

MONSIEUR VERDOUX (1947). With Marilyn Nash

doux, the polished bon vivant, the same man who employs one of the Tramp's oldest gags, pretending he is chasing a bee when someone discovers him making advances to Madame Grosnay? And is he the same man who, backing up apologetically, pratfalls out the window a second later? Still, almost everyone agrees that the slapstick sequences with Annabella provide the movie's most entertaining moments. In her gaudy dresses, with her loud, bovine manner, she has a vulgar élan that somehow defeats Verdoux's intensely cosmopolitan schemes; she remains unsinkable and unpoisonable. This characterization, however, owes as much to Martha Raye's wonderfully brassy performance as to Chaplin's conception.

In painful contrast to the Verdoux-Annabella escapades are the scenes with the homeless girl that Verdoux brings back to his apartment to kill. Only the conversation is deadly, however, as Chaplin uses it to expound his theories. Seeing that the girl is reading Schopenhauer, he suggests a gloomy view of life, from which suicide is the only escape. He is merely trying to ease his way in for the kill, however; it is clear he is far more in accord with her response: "Yet life is wonderful . . . Everything . . . a spring morning, a summer's night . . . music, art, love

. . ." As she reveals her marriage to a cripple, the counterpart to Verdoux's family ("I'd have killed for him," she says passionately), Verdoux sees that she is his philosophical twin. Aware of the misery of life, she also supports one of the basic theses of Verdoux's existence: "A little kindness can make it beautiful."

Many critics of *Monsieur Verdoux* have rejected its ideas as sophomoric and awkward. But, in actuality, it is only the expression of them that is callow. The metaphorical equation of killing and stealing with free enterprise is not too far removed, for instance, from a respected work like *The Threepenny Opera*. Furthermore, the flipside of this cynicism—Verdoux's humanistic and sensual disposition toward life—makes him a second cousin to any number of distinguished literary characters. (Overall, the Verdoux story is strikingly similar to Camus' novel, *The Stranger*.) The problem is that Chaplin launches his ideas at us from a nakedly didactic podium (the movie is practically a seminar), rather than allowing them to arise naturally from the events of his story.

And yet the groundwork for a solid dramatic structure seems to have been laid out. The miserable and impoverished Verdoux is not surprised to see the sardonic aspect of his philosophy borne out in his

LIMELIGHT (1952). With Claire Bloom

last encounter with the girl: she is now the mistress of a wealthy munitions manufacturer. In business he is "ruthless," she says, but to her he is "kind and generous." This sums up Verdoux's own duality, of course, but he focuses exclusively on the negative side. The girl, however, preaches his own gay, life-affirming attitude back at him. Thus, Chaplin cleverly splits the two halves of himself, the pessimistic and optimistic, and projects each into a different character.

The film is complex, then, but unfortunately very little of its complexity is realized in dramatic terms. This is partly the result of the talky, bloodless presentation it receives and partly a consequence of Chaplin's lethal infatuation with his spokesman Verdoux. The witty, elegant little philosopher moves serenely through a world of simpletons and ciphers; some he adroitly dupes and deceives (the women), others he neatly outpoints in intellectual duels (the priest). He is too insufferably, eternally "right" about everything to be dramatically viable—a problem with the movie that bears his name as well.

An even more acrid and autobiographically motivated Chaplin emerged in *Limelight* (1952). The furious misogyny of *Monsieur Verdoux* must have been intensified by the Joan Barry paternity case and by Chaplin's growing estrangement from American society.* The happiness of his marriage to Oona was not enough to offset these factors. From conception to execution, two and a half years went into *Limelight*, but the cost-conscious Chaplin kept the shooting time down to 50 days. Both American and European critics were quite warm towards the film, but its popular reception in this country was damaged by the American Legion's campaign to suppress it.

Set in London in 1914, *Limelight* concerns the relationship between Calvero (Chaplin), a once-famous clown who has lost his touch, and Terry (Claire Bloom), a ballerina whose psychological problems have paralyzed her legs. They meet when Calvero thwarts her suicide attempt in the shabby apartment house where they both live. They establish a pla-

Limelight also grew out of Chaplin's fascination with the neurotic and self-destructive tendencies of clowns. In his autobiography, he cites a long list of comics who committed suicide, in most cases because they had somehow lost touch with their audience. At another point he mentions Frank Tinney, a popular comedian of the pre-World War I era, whom Chaplin saw when he was at his height and then after his decline: "He was so self-conscious I could not believe it was the same man. It was this change in him that gave me the idea years later for my film *Limelight*." Unfortunately, Chaplin's own orientation, which is security-minded and self-enhancing, made him far from temperamentally ideal to explore the subject of self-destructiveness.

LIMELIGHT (1952). With Buster Keaton

tonic rooming arrangement and gradually Calvero helps the girl to regain her health. Terry gets a job with a ballet company and persuades the director to employ Calvero as a clown. The composer of the ballet (Sydney Chaplin), a handsome young man whom Terry knows from earlier, poorer days, falls in love with her, but she thinks only of Calvero. However, dissatisfaction with Calvero's performance causes him to leave the company abruptly. Some time later, the composer discovers Calvero with a group of drunken street musicians and manages to arrange a benefit performance for him. Unexpectedly, the performance is a great personal triumph for Calvero, who regains his old form. Immediately afterwards, however, he succumbs to a heart attack, while Terry dances a finale to the evening.

In its barest skeletal outline, *Limelight* is the profound work that Chaplin intended. Moreover, it is Chaplin's most personal film. In mild permutations, it showcases the various facets of Chaplin's long career: his triumphs as a pure clown; the growing sobriety and intellectual pretensions that alienated his audience; his marital problems (Calvero with five ex-wives is two up on Chaplin); the vice that helped blight his career (Calvero's drinking takes the place of Chaplin's romantic escapades). Conceptually, the film is also interesting in that it returns Chaplin-Calvero to his origins—the English music hall. In this context, the "elegant melancholy of twilight" of which Calvero speaks is deeply meaningful and affecting, the lyrics—so to speak—of Calvero's swan song.

But all this remains green potential that never ripens. The relationship between the performer and his audience never gets out of the declamatory stage and into the lifeblood of the story. Calvero expatiates endlessly on the mixture of love and hate he feels for his public; there is excoriation, affection and need reflected in his words. But the words never become actions (or interactions, for that matter; it's all Chaplin, intoning monologues) and the ideas never become drama.

The betrayal of possibilities results in the fact that, as with *Verdoux*, Chaplin is too corruptingly close to his creation: there is no distancing, no irony. The self-infatuation of Calvero is simply Chaplin gazing lovingly at himself in the mirror. Despite his ac-knowledged vices, the old clown is kind to the crippled girl; he is her deliverer, in fact. Unlike the libidinous Chaplin, his interest is fatherly; it is *she* who professes romantic ardor. Why not? Like Verdoux, Calvero is everything a girl could hope for in a father figure: worldly, refined, sensitive, compassionate, supportive. As for his failure with the public, this is scarcely his fault. Calvero makes it quite plain—and Chaplin does nothing to contradict him—that audiences are simply too obtuse to appreciate him.

But the real reason for Calvero's self-glorification is his bottomless wisdom. During the course of the film, he extemporizes in many keys, all of them heavily sententious. Some of the subjects he touches on are the mind (". . . this greatest toy ever invented"), time (" . . . the great author—he always writes the perfect ending") and self-hate ("We all despise ourselves"). The main burden of his philosophy, however, is conveyed in windy exhortations that somehow serve as Terry's therapy. "Life is not a meaning, it is a desire," he tells her. Although existence is freighted with miseries and disappointments, we must struggle to wrest momentary pleasure and happiness from it. Beyond this, a deeper satisfaction is available to artists, who can, through endless toil and self-sacrifice, know the

LIMELIGHT (1952). Calvero performs at the music hall

joy of creative achievement. It is artistic frustration and despair that has crippled Terry, and Calvero's inspiring monologues ultimately cure her disability and send her forth to become a great ballerina. "You are a true artist," he informs her after a performance, "a true artist."

As with *Monsieur Verdoux*, the critics are wrong in condemning Chaplin's philosophy outright. It isn't inherently any more simplistic than Luis Buñuel's notion of the universal vanity and cruelty of mankind or, to switch art forms, Henry James' concept of the unlived life, In fact, many of Calvero's yea-saying pronouncements could have come directly from James' greatest novel, *The Ambassadors*. But, unlike that novel, *Limelight* fails to provide its ideas with the invigorating quality of credible human situations and so they remain lifeless.

There are still other respects in which *Limelight* troubles and displeases. The mise-en-scène, a few paltry sets intended to simulate Georgian England, is claustrophobic. Recognizing no limits to his expanding ego, Chaplin insisted on supplying a ballet, *The Death of Columbine*, which is almost as inadequate as the lachrymose late-Romantic score, also supplied by Chaplin (though one theme became the popular hit "Eternally").

Apart from the intriguing revelations that *Limelight* provides about its creator, the film's only excuse for being is its four music-hall numbers, of which three occur in Calvero's dreams and the fourth is the encore at his benefit. The latter, in which Calvero is joined by his old partner (Buster Keaton), is the most ingratiating. The two old clowns remind us, if only fleetingly, of the kind of baggy-pants greatness they were once capable of. In what amounts to an allegory of the whole film, they slowly destroy their instruments (a piano and a violin), as if saying good-bye to their art. They are unable to complete the task, however, and finish in a joyous burst of fiddling and pounding. It is just about the only joy available in *Limelight*.

A King in New York, released in 1957, was the first Chaplin film since 1918 that was not produced at his own studio in Hollywood. An exile now, he was forced to work in England. The film was not shown in this country until 1973, at which time the unfavorable notices harmonized closely with the disappointment registered by English and French reviewers in 1957. However, no one could deny that, intellectually, Chaplin pulled in his horns with this one, retreating from his grand philosophical stance to social and political satire. He has rather disingenuously denied that

A KING IN NEW YORK (1957). With Joan Ingram and Dawn Addams

the movie is a parody of mid-century America, but a plot summary leaves no doubt which way the rapier was pointed.

Revolution forces King Shahdov (Chaplin) to flee from his kingdom, Estrovia, to New York, where he finds himself bankrupt. Against his better judgment, he lets a glib, attractive advertising woman (Dawn Addams) sign him up to do television commercials, some of which he bungles badly. To enhance his appeal, the girl persuades him to undergo cosmetic surgery, but he is unhappy with his new face and has the old one restored. His life becomes still more complicated when a boy prodigy (Michael Chaplin) takes refuge with him after the boy's parents are jailed as subversives. This results in a confrontation between the King and the House Un-American Activities Committee, which ends with the King accidentally hosing them down. Ulti-

A KING IN NEW YORK (1957). With Dawn Addams

mately, the boy is persuaded to cooperate with the committee in order to save his parents. This caps the king's growing disenchantment with the United States and he decides to rejoin his estranged wife in Europe.

The targets of Chaplin's satire are large, difficult to miss and not without a few punctures already: Madison Avenue, television, plastic surgery, and so on. Nevertheless, some of the humor, though perish-ably topical, comes off quite well. At a dinner party, the advertising woman maneuvers Shahdov into an amusing state of anxiety over the possibility of bad breath or body odor. After his plastic surgery, he attends a nightclub act and is forced to sit in an agony of muscle constriction amidst a roaring audience, lest he break the stitches on his face. The film's one truly outstanding sequence comes early in the story. In a restaurant, the savage din of a combo prevents the king from ordering and suddenly the great pantomimist of *City Lights* and *The Gold Rush* returns for a few seconds, as Shahdov ingeniously mimes his request for caviar and turtle soup.

Sadly, however, the fun in *A King in New York* comes at very infrequent intervals. A scene at a progressive school disintegrates into foolish slapstick, as does the HUAC hearing. In this latter sequence, where incisive satire is desperately needed, Chaplin reaches back to the days of *A Film Johnnie* for a fire hose. The part of the Madison Avenue girl is of some interest, since here at last is a feminine lead in a Chaplin film who is not crippled, blind or impoverished—but the interest is largely historical and biographical, not artistic. The inevitable Chaplin pathos might have added something as well, but the relationship between Shahdov and the boy prodigy is only a fatigued echo of the energetic schmaltz of *The Kid*.

Although there is probably no critic alive who would rank *A King in New York* above *Monsieur Verdoux* or *Limelight*, the film is something of a relief after these two previous Chaplins. However worthy of discussion they may be, they remain irredeemably turgid and self-rapt in a way that this superficial comedy is not. Of course it is hard to miss the symbolism of the exiled king who is vilified and persecuted in his adopted country. Still, the self-satisfaction of the film is nowhere near as towering as in the two earlier ventures. The king does not fall on the thorns of life as noisily as Verdoux or Calvero.

As all but his most fanatic admirers would concede, Chaplin's work has followed a long, gloomy downward arc since 1931. There are two different diagnoses for Chaplin's decline: that the would-be intellectual in Chaplin upstaged the entertainer and that his powers were simply on the wane and nothing could have reversed the process. Whatever their validity, neither of these explanations diminishes the fact that Chaplin's descent began at an unequaled height of creative achievement and if the stages of his deterioration included *Modern Times* and *The Great Dictator,* he was still a head or two above everyone else on the way down.

By 1966 marital happiness, renewed popularity and time had assuaged most of Chaplin's rancor toward the United States and he was more than willing to accept $4,000,000 from Universal to make a new film, *A Countess from Hong Kong*. The germ of the story was planted on Chaplin's 1931 trip to Shanghai, where he came into contact with a number of White Russian aristocrats who had fled to China at the time of the revolution and were living in the grimmest of poverty. Out of this background, Chaplin developed a script (he had actually begun it in 1940) that he was able to shoot in 50 days, despite having to work with two highly temperamental and incompatible stars, Marlon Brando and Sophia Loren. It is a tribute to his awesome mystique that he was able to get absolute cooperation out of them. (He himself shows up very briefly as a steward, this being only the second film in his career in which he did not play a sizable role.) Most critics were not impressed, however, and the unkind notices practically suggested that Chaplin was senile.

The film's tone is gentle and beneficent, even sweet-tempered. It is basically a bedroom farce involving a dance-hall girl from Hong Kong and a millionaire diplomat. The daughter of devastated Russian émigrés, Natascha (Sophia Loren) spends the night with Ogden Mears

SWAN SONG AND SUMMING UP

(Marlon Brando). She likes him (and his money) so much that when she hears he is sailing to Saudi Arabia to become the new ambassador, she stows away in his stateroom. The bulk of the film is taken up with Mears' efforts to avoid a scandal and Natascha's campaign to make him fall in love with her. Along the way to a conventional happy ending, there are a lot of familiar ingredients: Mears' loyal buddy Harvey (Sydney Chaplin); a bitchy Mrs. Mears (Tippi Hedren) to play foil to Natascha; an attempt to arouse Mears' jealousy at a shipboard ball; a lecherous, pesky fellow named Felix (Michael Medwin) who emerges from Natascha's past and almost upsets the apple cart.

The film is deficient in a way that most assembly-line Hollywood products rarely are, without having the compensating pleasure that set Chaplin's best work apart. There are two wrenchingly abrupt transitions, for instance, which serve to confuse and alienate the audience. The film also suffers from the atmosphere of Scrooge-like economy that haunts so many of Chaplin's movies. For ambiance, he asks us to be content with a few "establishing shots" of Hong Kong. Later, on board the ship, he inserts, with computerlike regularity, alternat-

A COUNTESS FROM HONG KONG (1967). With Sophia Loren and Marlon Brando

A COUNTESS FROM HONG KONG (1967). Chaplin directing Sophia Loren and Marlon Brando

ing shots of the ocean by day and by night.

On the other hand, if one's expectations are lowered to a normal level, *A Countess from Hong Kong* has its charms. The pacing of the major comic episodes is brisk, with the principals rushing about mugging wildly and waving their arms. Mears attempts to conceal Natascha's presence, Natascha coyly drags her feet, countless confusions and misunderstandings develop, all to the staccato accompaniment of slamming doors. A couple of sequences involving insipid ingenues don't quite come off, but a set piece with Margaret Rutherford as a dotty old ship's passenger works well. A later scene at the bar with Mears, Natascha, Harvey and Felix looks for a moment as if it will develop into a classic vaudeville turn of some sort, but Chaplin doesn't carry it past an initial gag or two.

The two stars hit and maintain the proper farcical mood and most of the film is indistinguishable from any competently played sex comedy. In the interstices of the romping and running, however, some characteristic Chaplin moments do bloom. A few scattered comments about Natascha's poverty-stricken upbringing remind us of other deprived Chaplin heroines, while the

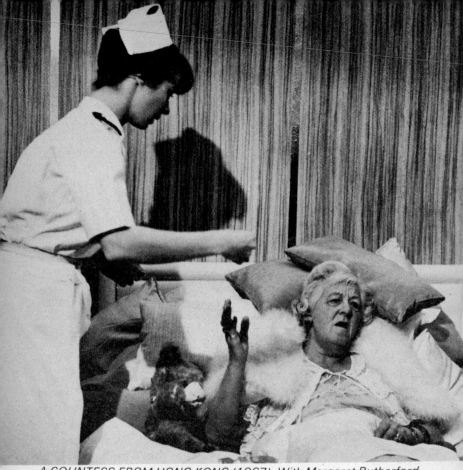

A COUNTESS FROM HONG KONG (1967). With Margaret Rutherford

ill-fitting clothes she is forced to wear at different points remind us of Chaplin himself. In addition, there is a quality of lovely sadness to the opening scene, in which declassed patrician beauties parade themselves in a dance hall. Later, in a restaurant sequence, Natascha and two courtesan companions return to their table from the powder room with a stately and elegant tread.

* * * * *

Appraisals of Chaplin's career vary from George Jean Nathan's 1931 attempt to cut him down to size (to a "professional zany," to be exact) to the worshipful litanies of Peter Cotes, Thelma Niklaus, Robert Payne, Emil Ludwig and other critics whose idolatry of Chaplin, it would seem, stops just short of human sacrifice. In this sect, the largest quantities of incense are burned by Ludwig, who thinks of Chaplin as a man "who has shaken the world as only the figure of Christ has done before him," and Peter Cotes, who deems him the "First Artist of our times." Among critics who do not view Chaplin's work from the perspective of a church pew, there are, of course, many shades of opinion other than Nathan's. But there is a good deal more awe than disparagement registered in the essays on Chaplin by, say, Gilbert Seldes, Eric Bentley, and Bosley Crowther.

To supply some critical ballast to the lopsided discussions of Chaplin's work, it is probably best to start with what he did not accomplish rather than what he did. First, Chaplin was not, as Gerith von Ulm designated him, the "King of Tragedy"—nor even the earl, the duke or some lesser peer of the realm. The human misery Chaplin incorporated into his films may reflect tragedy in the journalistic sense of the term, but it is unrelated to the literary mode of that name. As perfected by Sophocles and Shakespeare, it can never be fully divorced from its old trappings —the downfall of a man of high station, pride and guilt, the tragic flaw, the final awakening. Chaplin's films do not even begin to fit the def-

inition of this much-abused term because they are seldom touched by inner conflict of any sort.* Neither the Tramp nor the suffering creature he helps exhibit any ambivalence or divided feelings, nor do they bear any measure of guilt for their predicament, as a tragic hero should. Fate, society and environmental factors are generally the culprits in Chaplin's work. For him, tragedy may mean the debilitations of poverty or blindness or paralysis, but there is no reason why it has to mean that to us.

Another myth about Chaplin that must be rejected is his directorial expertise. Cotes and Niklaus gush over his handling of actors, quoting Else Codd, one of his early secretaries, as follows: " . . . without exaggeration, I think I can say he has played every character in every one of his comedies." They add that "he whipped his players into a state of excitement that made them give their best." This is a sad commentary on Chaplin's actors, who turned in a series of commonplace performances reaching all the way back to the comedian's earliest days. There are, for instance, villains from Bud Jamison (*The Tramp*) to Allan Garcia (*The Cir-*

* The only possible exception in the Chaplin canon is *A Woman of Paris*, but even its applicability is doubtful, since the real focus of the movie is the relationship of Marie and Pierre, not Jean.

CITY LIGHTS (1931). As the Little Tramp

cus) to the members of HUAC (*A King in New York*) and leading men from Lloyd Bacon (*The Vagabond*) to Malcolm Waite (*The Gold Rush*) to Sydney Chaplin (*Limelight*). But there is not much to praise or blame in these performances and it is not surprising that very few of Chaplin's actors went on to independent careers. Of course, a good deal of the blame must go to him; he peopled his movies with stock characters, creatures of limited emotional resources who would never threaten the Tramp's primacy. The chief exceptions are the simple but expressive parts assigned to Mack Swain and Eric Campbell, types so antithetical to Chaplin that they could be permitted to display some talent and still remain foils for the Master. We have to conclude that, consciously or unconsciously, the strenuous perfectionism he imposed on his casts was mainly aimed at enhancing the quality of his own performance.*

This situation is most glaring in the case of Chaplin's heroines. They were almost all snatched from obscurity by him—his "discoveries" —only to be returned to darkness

---

* Again the exception is *A Woman of Paris*, that splendid anomaly of Chaplin's career, in which he was able, for once, to create memorable characters other than the Tramp and shape the acting to the parts with uniform brilliance.

after their brief reign as his new queen. One exception is Edna Purviance, with her heavily sedated acting style, who survived for eight years as Chaplin's leading lady. But in later years only Paulette Goddard could boast more than one film with Chaplin. His vanity was evidently so great that he thought he could take any lump of human clay and mold it into a "true artist." But however doggedly he sought to play Pygmalion, statues like Merna Kennedy and Virginia Cherrill stubbornly refused to come to life. Of them all, only Paulette Goddard had much of a career after leaving Chaplin, and only Claire Bloom went on to genuine distinction.

Occasionally, when circumstances demanded it, Chaplin used performers of proven ability (Martha Raye, Jack Oakie), but most of the time he preferred to spare himself the expense and the competition. He was probably happiest with his repertory company of loyal troupers like Henry Bergman, plodding along in submissive mediocrity through film after film because they didn't doubt for a minute their boss' conviction that the public was paying to see him. They were the orchestra; he was the conductor.

This dimension of Chaplin's work throws some additional light on the relative inferiority of his talking

THE GOLD RUSH (1925). Wistfully, Charlie watches Malcolm Waite and Georgia Hale.

films. Shocking as it may appear to the average film critic, most people expect less of silent movies than talkies, if only because actors in sound films carry a double burden —they have to be heard as well as seen. When a director is as careless as Chaplin was with Maurice Moscovich in *The Great Dictator*, with the entire Couvais family in *Monsieur Verdoux*, and with his own son Sydney in *Limelight*, the amateurish results are multiplied by two. It is common to complain about the stage-bound garrulousness and egoism of Chaplin's talking films, as if he suddenly began a second career in 1940, quite distinct from the first one in silent films. This proposition founders on the simple fact that Chaplin's solipsistic approach to filmmaking—reducing his secondary players to the status of foils whose existence is wholly dependent on him—is a constant in *all* his work, sound or silent. The only material difference is that in his silent films the actors are the butts of visual gags, whereas in the talking Chaplins they are skewered with verbal wit. The bullies and policemen who once played stooge for his acrobatic and pantomimic stunts are reincarnated in the priest (*Monsieur Verdoux*) and the Madison Avenue girl (*A King in New York*), who cooperatively feed him lines. Of course there is a considerable qualitative difference between these two categories; as everyone is agreed, Chaplin's genius is visual, not verbal.

At the technical end of filmmaking, Chaplin has always struck most observers as flat-footed, if not lame. Scornful of "Hollywood chichi," which he seems to define as any camerawork more elaborate than occasional cross-cutting, he is proud of his ability to keep the lighting, editing and cinematography in his films in a prehistoric state. However, since there is so much consensus on this point, it is useless to do more than call attention to a few instances of his ineptitude, such as the poor matching of studio and location shots in *The Gold Rush*, the churning train wheels that signal transitions in *Monsieur Verdoux*, the distinctly Londonish look of some of the shots in *A King in New York*, and the programmed glimpses of the sea in *A Countess from Hong Kong*.

There is somewhat more enthusiasm for Chaplin's music than his cinematic techniques. His interest in music dates from his earliest days, and he has often asserted that sequences in his films were influenced by an evocative melody he heard. Although lacking in formal training as a musician, he has taught himself to play several instruments. His first complete film score was for *City Lights* and from then on his "one-man-show" had a new act. He has even invaded his own past in

CITY LIGHTS (1931). Charlie returns home to Virginia Cherrill.

this regard, composing new music for most of his early films. Working closely with experienced musicians, he has hummed out scores that include rhumbas, tangos, noisy nightclub jazz, jaunty tunes to reinforce comic business, and lush romantic motifs. Regardless of tempo or dynamics, however, this music seriously overtaxes Chaplin's versatility. His earnestness (he spent nine months on the score of *Limelight*) is not enough to redeem the banal tunes he has conjured up. Whether it is the pseudo-cowboy number "Bound for Texas" (*The Pilgrim*), the cloyingly upbeat "Swing, Little Girl" (*The Circus*) or the crippled Tchaikovsky that accompanies his ballet (*Limelight*), Chaplin's music remains hopelessly derivative.

This, then, is the case against Chaplin. Much of the confusion in discerning his true worth—which certainly dwarfs his inadequacies —results from incautiously applying to his work terminology normally reserved for novelists and playwrights. Chaplin was not a practitioner of intellectual comedy like Shaw, or black humor like Evelyn Waugh, or comedy of manners like Wilde; subjecting his comparatively fragile work to the heavy artillery of university scholarship only produces ludicrous results (e.g., "Recurrent Patterns of Shoe Imagery in *The Gold Rush*"). Chaplin was a great popular entertainer, probably without peer in this century. The immense breadth and scope of his gifts as a performer have been extensively praised elsewhere in this book. By way of précis, we can merely note that these gifts range from the subtlest pantomime to the broadest slapstick, from nimble-footed pratfalls to finely cadenced movements that verge on ballet, from sleight-of-hand to breathtaking physical dexterity. If he was occasionally vulgar, he was more often spirited and endearing.

Through most of his career, Chaplin remained answerable chiefly to his vast public, which, despite his sojourns in the salons of London and Paris, was essentially the way he wanted it. However he may have thrilled highbrows and intellectuals and sought to associate himself with their world, his truest and deepest rapport was with the masses. In return for their adulation, he made them laugh with a gusto and a consistency that no one else could match. But even more than this, once his narrative skills ripened, he incarnated the most universal fantasies of his public; he gave them back their reveries in hilarious and touching forms. At the same time, he never ridiculed these dreams because he himself participated in them too fully to allow for a condescending tone. The Tramp's first simple longings—food, shelter, and escape from destitution—are the yearnings of Chaplin's own youth. When the scope of the clown's aspirations expands to include women, adventure, sudden wealth—this, too, is Chaplin. The endless succession of pretty, blank faces in his films leads back to Hetty Kelly, and the Tramp's many acts of heroism in the face of danger can be looked on as Chaplin's dreams of theatrical glory transmuted into a more universal form. In this sense, it is fitting that the Tramp's attractions to women are all purely physical (as Chaplin's was to Hetty); in popular culture, qualities of mind and character would be too prosy or too confusing to constitute an ideal.

Movies, it must be remembered, began as idle distraction for the lower middle class, little five-cent snatches of escapism for tired workmen. These harmless nickelodeon narcotics were the basic fare of American cinema for at least two decades. Aesthetic hand-me-downs from nineteenth-century England, they were what nurtured the imagination of early filmmakers, D.W. Griffith most prominently. In Chaplin's case, the melodramas of his stage experience (e.g., *East Lynne, Jimmy the Fearless*) were all

THE IDLE CLASS (1921). Trouble in the park

the art he knew. He was able to take them even more seriously than his public because for him these sentimentalized tales of poverty represented his own youth, while the poor, chaste, suffering heroines were his mother. (Later, in his films, her mental illness was transformed into the physical infirmities of some of his heroines.) The plays of Dion Boucicault and Augustus Daly were the maudlin paradigms to which he shaped his movies and in which he saw his own life. Their residuum was still discernible in *A King in New York* and *A Countess from Hong Kong.*

It was not sincerity, however, that saved Chaplin from joining the long gray line of aesthetic mediocrities around him (although, as has already been noted, Chaplin's inspiration seems to have burned most brightly when his subject matter was autobiographical). Rather it was his success at creating a hybrid of forms: melodrama tempered by comedy and frequently pathos. Associates with blinkered visions warned Chaplin about mixing genres, but he wisely followed his own instincts. As a result, he was able to renovate some of the creaky Victorian formulas about waifs and flower girls with fresh and original humor and touches of authentic—if limited—sensibility. The effectiveness of this sensibility in Chaplin's work depended on the discipline and control with which it was invoked and the extent to which Chaplin was able to detach himself from specific Victorian *plots*, as opposed to Victorian characters and situations that he incorporated into a modern context. For example, the basic framework of *The Kid* is a weepy melodrama with built-in tears; the responses are mechanical, predetermined by stock situations.

A discriminating audience would be right to resist such manipulation. Furthermore, in the turbulent scene in which the Tramp and the Kid fend off the villains from the orphan asylum, the acting and direction are as overblown as the material. In *The Gold Rush*, on the other hand, where the pathos emanates from the Tramp's loneliness and the girls' failure to honor his invitation, the motivations approximate realism and plausibility.

Chaplin not only ascended to the very peak of popular mythology, he created a new peak, since the Tramp was a true original. In spite of his indebtedness to Commedia

LIMELIGHT (1952). Calvero and his friends attend the bedridden Terry (Claire Bloom).

MODERN TIMES (1936). A rare joyful moment with the machinery

dell' Arte figures like Pierrot and Harlequin, and to some of Chaplin's music-hall predecessors like Max Linder, there was never anything quite like him before. Although Agee inflates him rather absurdly by saying "he is as centrally representative of humanity . . . as Hamlet," he is probably the most famous and admired character that popular culture has produced in this country. He has been compared to Joyce's Leopold Bloom, who probably holds this rank for literature during the same time span. The parallels are strong—both characters are noteworthy for their alienation from society, their social insecurity, their heroic daydreams, their lack of imposing physical and psychological features, their gentleness. Yet Charlie's life is largely external, a battle against unsympathetic giants to obtain romance and wealth, while Bloom's life is internal, a welter of conflicts and inaction. Also, Joyce leaves Bloom pretty much where he found him—his tensions unresolved; Chaplin more often than not prefers a happy resolution to the Tramp's quest. (There is a common misconception—even among film critics—that Chaplin's movies often end unhappily; actually between *The Tramp* in 1915 and *Monsieur Verdoux* in 1947, this is true in only three or four films.)

Here, then, is another mandate of popular culture in the United States. The American public does not respond well to unhappy endings. As it happens, until his late, embittered period, Chaplin doesn't seem to have cared much for them either. So, apart from *The Circus* and a few other films where he sent the Tramp down a long, empty road, Chaplin was only too happy to oblige in this regard. It is yet another area in which he and his vast public were in perfect accord. In his unrelenting devotion to the theatrical forms they could best relate to, in his scrupulous avoidance of the esoteric and the complex, in his spirited, innovative renderings of popular myths about romance and heroism, in his limitless comic fertility—in all these respects, Chaplin, the King of Comedy, definitely earned his crown. His kingdom, the popular arts, was strictly one of surfaces, not flickering depths or latticed intricacies, but like Sir Cecil in *The Rink*, he glided across them with incomparable ease.

Under the circumstances, the vast scope of his influence should come as a surprise to no one. Although his own work shows the impact of some of his contemporaries (e.g., Harold Lloyd), he was far more a leader than a follower. To the long list of Chaplin gags that later saw service with other comedians may be added the mirror se-

CITY LIGHTS (1931). Charlie dreams of the girl (Virginia Cherrill).

quence in *The Floorwalker* (used by the Marx Brothers in *Duck Soup*), the "puppeteering" in *A Dog's Life* (reemployed by Laurel and Hardy in *A Chump at Oxford*) and the arboreal disguise in *Shoulder Arms* (an ancestor of Woody Allen's robot outfit in *Sleeper*). Moreover, *The Great Dictator*, Chaplin's one creditable effort at playing doubles, looks like the archetype for Danny Kaye's entire career, which has consistently exploited the same device in similar ways (e.g., *Wonder Man*, *Knock on Wood*, *On the Double*). Chaplin's artistic interaction with his contemporaries took an ironic turn when the producers of René Clair's *À Nous la Liberté*, which contained a satire on the industrial age that undoubtedly influenced Chaplin's *Modern Times*, sued Chaplin for plagiarism. Clair crippled his producers' case, however, by declaring that he himself had often borrowed from Chaplin!

Chaplin has been accused of just about everything; in addition to plagiarism, charges of mean-spiritedness, towering egoism, greed, and lack of generosity in acknowledging other people's achievements have been leveled against him. There is probably some truth to all these accusations. But they are rather small truths compared to the colossal verity of his accomplishments. As has been suggested earlier, the quality of Chaplin's films can sometimes be questioned but rarely their integrity. Against the bland technology of Hollywood's factory system, he set the lonely dedication of individual genius and maintained that stance for forty years. Against the impersonalism of machine-produced movies, he set the deep emotional commitment of a personal vision and autobiographical subject matter—qualities so common in the serious arts and so rare in mass culture. If the ultimate consequences of these attributes included self-indulgent, wrong-headed endeavors like *Limelight* and *Monsieur Verdoux*, this was long after they had given us *A Dog's Life*, *Shoulder Arms*, *The Gold Rush* and *City Lights*. His primitive techniques, lapses of taste, and self-involvement prove there are no gods among us; but, at his most sublime, his inspired comedy, delicacy of touch and uncompromising artistry shows us that there are certainly giants.

BIBLIOGRAPHY

Books

Agee, James. *Agee on Film*. Grosset & Dunlap, New York, 1958.

Bentley, Eric. *In Search of Theater*. Vintage Books, New York, 1954.

Chaplin, Charles. *My Autobiography*. Simon and Schuster, New York, 1964.

——————. *My Wonderful Visit*. Hurst and Blackett, London, 1922.

Cotes, Peter and Thelma Niklaus. *The Little Fellow*. The Citadel Press, New York, 1965.

Delluc, Louis. *Charlie Chaplin*. (Translated by Hamish Miles) Bodley Head, London, 1922.

Durgnat, Raymond. *The Crazy Mirror; Hollywood Comedy and the American Image*. Faber and Faber, London, 1969.

Huff, Theodore. *Charlie Chaplin*. Pyramid Books, New York, 1964.

McCaffrey, Donald (ed.). *Focus On Chaplin*. Prentice-Hall, Englewood Cliffs, N.J., 1971.

Macdonald, Dwight. *Dwight Macdonald On Movies*. Prentice-Hall, Englewood Cliffs, N.J., 1969.

McDonald, Gerald D. *The Films of Charlie Chaplin*. The Citadel Press, New York, 1965.

Payne, Robert. *The Great God Pan; a Biography of the Tramp Played By Charles Chaplin*. Hermitage House, New York, 1952.

Quigly, Isabel. *Charlie Chaplin; Early Comedies*. Studio Vista/Dutton Pictureback, London, 1968.

Tyler, Parker. *Chaplin, Last of the Clowns*. Horizon, New York, 1972.

——————. *Magic and Myth of the Movies*. Henry Holt, New York, 1947.

Von Ulm, Gerith. *Chaplin, King of Tragedy*. Caxton Printers, Caldwell, Idaho, 1940.

Articles

Capp, Al. "The Comedy of Charlie Chaplin." *Atlantic Monthly* (February 1950).

Charlie Chaplin: "Facts and Facets." *Film Comment*. (September-October, 1972): Twelve essays on Chaplin by different critics.

Hickey, Terry. "Accusations Against Charles Chaplin for Political and Moral Offenses." *Film Comment* (Winter 1969).

Seldes, Gilbert. "A Chaplin Masterpiece." *The New Republic* (February 25, 1931).

Spears, Jack. "Chaplin's Collaborators." *Films in Review* (January 1962).

Van Doren, Mark. "Charlie Chaplin." *The Nation* (February 18, 1936).

Wilson, Edmund. "The New Chaplin Comedy." *The New Republic* (September 2, 1925).

Young, Stark. "Dear Mr. Chaplin." *The New Republic* (August 23, 1922).

THE FILMS OF CHARLIE CHAPLIN

In much of his early work at Keystone, Chaplin had no hand in the writing or direction of his films; in other cases he collaborated with other members of the Keystone staff. In these instances, the relevant name (or names) appears after the title below. With the exception of *Tillie's Punctured Romance*, Chaplin wrote and directed all his films from *Caught In A Cabaret* to his most recent effort, *A Countess From Hong Kong*.

Keystone Films (1914)

MAKING A LIVING (1 reel). *Henry Lehrman*. Cast: Henry Lehrman, Chester Conklin.

KID AUTO RACES AT VENICE (half reel). *Henry Lehrman*. Cast: Henry Lehrman, Charlotte Fitzpatrick.

MABEL'S STRANGE PREDICAMENT (1 reel). *Henry Lehrman and Mack Sennett*. Cast: Mabel Normand, Chester Conklin, Alice Davenport.

BETWEEN THE SHOWERS (1 reel). *Henry Lehrman*. Cast: Ford Sterling, Chester Conklin.

A FILM JOHNNIE (1 reel). *Henry Lehrman*. Cast: Fatty Arbuckle, Minta Durfee.

TANGO TANGLES (1 reel). *Mack Sennett*. Cast: Ford Sterling, Fatty Arbuckle.

HIS FAVORITE PASTIME (1 reel). *George Nichols*. Cast: Peggy Pearce, Fatty Arbuckle.

CRUEL, CRUEL LOVE (1 reel). *George Nichols*. Cast: Chester Conklin, Alice Davenport, Minta Durfee.

THE STAR BOARDER (1 reel). *Mack Sennett*. Cast: Edgar Kennedy, Alice Davenport.

MABEL AT THE WHEEL (2 reels). *Mack Sennett and Mabel Normand*. Cast: Mabel Normand, Chester Conklin.

TWENTY MINUTES OF LOVE (1 reel). *Mack Sennett*. Cast: Edgar Kennedy, Chester Conklin, Minta Durfee.

CAUGHT IN A CABARET (2 reels). *Mabel Normand and Charles Chaplin*. Cast: Mabel Normand, Mack Swain, Alice Davenport.

CAUGHT IN THE RAIN (1 reel). Cast: Alice Davenport, Mack Swain.

A BUSY DAY (half reel). Cast: Mack Swain.

THE FATAL MALLET (1 reel). Cast: Mabel Normand, Mack Sennett.

HER FRIEND THE BANDIT (1 reel). *Charles Chaplin and Mabel Normand*. Cast: Mabel Normand, Charles Murray.

THE KNOCKOUT (2 reels). *Mack Sennett*. Cast: Fatty Arbuckle, Slim Summerville.

MABEL'S BUSY DAY (1 reel). *Mabel Normand and Charles Chaplin*. Cast: Mabel Normand, Chester Conklin.

MABEL'S MARRIED LIFE (1 reel). *Charles Chaplin and Mabel Normand*. Cast: Mabel Normand, Mack Swain.

LAUGHING GAS (1 reel). Cast: Fritz Schade, Slim Summerville.

THE PROPERTY MAN (2 reels). Cast: Fritz Schade, Phyllis Allen.

THE FACE ON THE BARROOM FLOOR (1 reel). Cast: Fritz Schade, Chester Conklin.

RECREATION (half reel). Cast: Charles Chaplin.

THE MASQUERADER (1 reel). Cast: Fatty Arbuckle, Minta Durfee.

HIS NEW PROFESSION (1 reel). Cast: Charles Chase, Minta Durfee.

THE ROUNDERS (1 reel). Cast: Fatty Arbuckle, Al St. John.

THE NEW JANITOR (1 reel). Cast: Al St. John, Fritz Schade.

THOSE LOVE PANGS (1 reel). Cast: Chester Conklin, Cecile Arnold.

DOUGH AND DYNAMITE (2 reels). Cast: Chester Conklin, Slim Summerville.

GENTLEMEN OF NERVE (1 reel). Cast: Mabel Normand, Chester Conklin.

HIS MUSICAL CAREER (1 reel). Cast: Mack Swain, Alice Howell.

HIS TRYSTING PLACE (2 reels). Cast: Mabel Normand, Mack Swain.

TILLIE'S PUNCTURED ROMANCE (6 reels). *Mack Sennett,* based on *Tillie's Nightmare*, by Edgar Smith. Cast: Marie Dressler, Mabel Normand, Mack Swain.

GETTING ACQUAINTED (1 reel). Phyllis Allen, Mabel Normand, Mack Swain.

HIS PREHISTORIC PAST (2 reels). Cast: Mack Swain, Fritz Schade.

Essanay Films (1915)

HIS NEW JOB (2 reels). Cast: Ben Turpin, Leo White.

A NIGHT OUT (2 reels). Cast: Ben Turpin, Bud Jamison.

THE CHAMPION (2 reels). Cast: Bud Jamison, Edna Purviance.

IN THE PARK (1 reel). Cast: Edna Purviance, Leo White.

THE JITNEY ELOPEMENT (2 reels). Cast: Edna Purviance, Leo White.

THE TRAMP (2 reels). Cast: Bud Jamison, Edna Purviance.

BY THE SEA (1 reel). Cast: Edna Purviance, Billy Armstrong.

WORK (2 reels). Cast: Charles Insley, Edna Purviance, Marta Golden.

A WOMAN (2 reels). Cast: Edna Purviance, Leo White.

THE BANK (2 reels). Cast: Edna Purviance, Billy Armstrong.

SHANGHAIED (2 reels). Cast: Edna Purviance, Wesley Ruggles.

A NIGHT AT THE SHOW (2 reels). Cast: Edna Purviance, Leo White.

CARMEN (4 reels). Cast: Edna Purviance, Ben Turpin.

POLICE (2 reels). Cast: Edna Purviance, Leo White, Wesley Ruggles.

TRIPLE TROUBLE (2 reels). Cast: Edna Purviance, Billy Armstrong.

Mutual Films (1916-17)

THE FLOORWALKER (2 reels). Cast: Edna Purviance, Lloyd Bacon, Eric Campbell.

THE FIREMAN (2 reels). Cast: Edna Purviance, Eric Campbell, Lloyd Bacon.

THE VAGABOND (2 reels). Cast: Edna Purviance, Lloyd Bacon.

ONE A.M. (2 reels). Cast: Charles Chaplin.

THE COUNT (2 reels). Cast: Edna Purviance, Eric Campbell.

THE PAWNSHOP (2 reels). Cast: Edna Purviance, Henry Bergman.

BEHIND THE SCREEN (2 reels). Cast: Eric Campbell, Edna Purviance.

THR RINK (2 reels). Cast: Edna Purviance, Eric Campbell, Henry Bergman.

EASY STREET (2 reels). Cast: Edna Purviance, Eric Campbell.

THE CURE (2 reels). Cast: Edna Purviance, Eric Campbell.

THE IMMIGRANT (2 reels). Cast: Edna Purviance, Eric Campbell.

THE ADVENTURER (2 reels). Cast: Edna Purviance, Eric Campbell.

First National Films (1918-22)

A DOG'S LIFE (3 reels). Cast: Edna Purviance, Albert Austin, Chuck Riesner.

THE BOND (half reel). Cast: Albert Austin, Edna Purviance.

SHOULDER ARMS (3 reels). Cast: Edna Purviance, Henry Bergman, Sidney Chaplin.

SUNNYSIDE (3 reels). Cast: Edna Purviance, Henry Bergman.

A DAY'S PLEASURE (2 reels). Cast: Edna Purviance, Henry Bergman.

THE KID (6 reels). Cast: Jackie Coogan, Edna Purviance, Chuck Riesner.

THE IDLE CLASS (2 reels). Cast: Edna Purviance, Mack Swain.

PAY DAY (2 reels). Cast: Mack Swain, Edna Purviance.

THE PILGRIM (4 reels). Cast: Edna Purviance, Mack Swain, Tom Murray.

United Artists (1923-1952)

A WOMAN OF PARIS. Cast: Carl Miller, Adolphe Menjou, Edna Purviance, Lydia Knott. (1923)

THE GOLD RUSH. Cast: Mack Swain, Tom Murray, Georgia Hale, Malcolm Waite. (1925)

THE CIRCUS. Cast: Merna Kennedy, Harry Crocker, Allan Garcia, Henry Bergman. (1928)

CITY LIGHTS. Cast: Virginia Cherrill, Harry Meyers, Henry Bergman. (1931)

MODERN TIMES. Cast: Paulette Goddard, Henry Bergman, Chester Conklin, Allan Garcia. (1936)

THE GREAT DICTATOR. Cast: Paulette Goddard, Jack Oakie, Reginald Gardiner, Henry Daniell, Billy Gilbert, Maurice Moscovich. (1940)

MONSIEUR VERDOUX. Cast: Martha Raye, Mady Correll, Margaret Hoffman, Marilyn Nash, William Frawley. (1947)

LIMELIGHT. Cast: Claire Bloom, Sydney Chaplin, Nigel Bruce, Buster Keaton. (1952)

Late Films

A KING IN NEW YORK. Archway. Cast: Dawn Addams, Michael Chaplin, Oliver Johnston. (1957)

A COUNTESS FROM HONG KONG. Universal. Cast: Marlon Brando, Sophia Loren, Syndey Chaplin, Margaret Rutherford. (1967)

INDEX

Addams, Dawn, 126, 217
Adventurer, The, 33, 60-61, 63
Agee, James, 113, 143
Allen, Woody, 145
A Nous la Liberté, 145
Arbuckle, Fatty, 24, 27, 31, 35
Arnold, Cecile, 27
Austin, Albert, 44

Bacon, Lloyd, 135
Baker, Nellie Bly, 76
Bank, The, 36, 37, 39
Barrie, Sir James, 17, 73
Barry, Joan, 21, 121
Battling Butler, 39
Behind the Screen, 49, 51
Bentley, Eric, 133
Bergman, Henry, 43, 49, 55, 95, 135
Between the Showers, 26
Bloom, Claire, 21, 120, 121, 135
Boucicault, Dion, 140
Brando, Marlon, 129, 130, 131
Broadway After Dark, 87
Buñuel, Luis, 125
Bushman, Francis X., 37
By the Sea, 35

Caesar, Sid, 96
Campbell, Eric, 43, 52, 54, 56, 58, 61, 79, 135
Camus, Albert, *The Stranger,* 119
Carey, Gary, 72
Carmen burlesque, 37, 39
Caught in a Cabaret, 33
Caught in the Rain, 29
Champion, The, 39, 40
Chaplin, Charles, Jr. (Charles Chaplin's son), 19
Chaplin, Charles, Sr. (Charles Chaplin's father), 12

Chaplin, Hannah (Lily Harley) (Charles Chaplin's mother), 12, 17
Chaplin, Michael (Charles Chaplin's son), 126
Chaplin, Sydney (Charles Chaplin's half-brother), 12-14, 65
Chaplin, Sydney (Charles Chaplin's son), 19, 122, 135, 137
Cherrill, Virginia, 98, 99, 100, 101, 135, 138
Chump at Oxford, A, 145
Circus, The, 45, 47, 91, 93, 94-97, 133-135, 138, 143
City Lights, 19, 39, 45, 96, 97-102, 103, 128, 134, 137, 138, 144, 145
Clair, René, 145
Clifton, Emma, 26
Codd, Else, 133
Conklin, Chester, 26, 29, 31, 49, 108
Coogan, Jackie, 69, 74
Correll, Mady, 113
Cotes, Peter, and Thelma Niklaus, *The Little Fellow,* 111 and n., 132, 133
Count, The, 47, 49, 52, 60, 75
Countess from Hong Kong, A, 21, 129-132, 137, 140
Court Jester, The, 37
Couvais, Thelma, 113
Crocker, Harry, 94
Crowther, Bosley, 133
Cruel, Cruel Love, 29
Cure, The, 54, 56, 58, 63

Daly, Augustin, 140
Daniell, Henry, 110
d'Arrast, Henry d'Abbadie, 86
Davis, Robert O., 115
Day's Pleasure, A, 69, 72
Delluc, Louis, *Charlie Chaplin,* 11
DeMille, Cecil B., 86
Dog's Life, A, 63, 64, 66, 77, 105, 145

Dough and Dynamite, 29
Dressler, Marie, 30
Duck Soup, 145

Easy Street, 14, 51-52, 54, 57, 105
Eight Lancashire Lads, 12
Eisler, Hans, 21
Edwards, Vivian, 27

Face on the Barroom Floor, The, 27, 29
Fairbanks, Douglas, 15, 67
Fatal Mallet, The, 29
Fields, W.C., 67n.
Film Johnnie, A, 29, 128
Fireman, The, 43, 44, 45
Floorwalker, The, 43, 145
Foster, W.C., 43

Garcia, Allan, 93, 94, 133
Gardiner, Reginald, 107, 115
Gentleman of Paris, A, 87
Gentlemen of Nerve, 31
George, Lloyd, 19
Getting Acquainted, 26
Gilbert, Billy, 110
Glyn, Elinor, 16
Goddard, Paulette (Mrs. Charles Chaplin),
    18, 19, 103, 104, 107, 111, 114, 135
Gold Rush, The, 19, 86, 87, 89, 90, 92, 94,
    128, 135, 136, 137, 139, 145
Goodwin, Fred, 38

Great Dictator, The, 19, 107, 109-112, 114,
    115, 128, 136, 145
Grey, Lita (Mrs. Charles Chaplin), 16, 19, 94
Griffith, D.W., 15, 86, 139

Hale, Georgia, 89, 90, 136
Hardy, Thomas, 87
Harris, Mildred (Mrs. Charles Chaplin), 17,
    19, 71

Hedren, Tippi, 129
Her Friend the Bandit, 33
His Favorite Pastime, 27
His Musical Profession, 29
His New Job, 34, 35, 37
His New Profession, 29
His Prehistoric Past, 29, 33
His Trysting Place, 28, 31
Hitler, Adolf, 107, 111
Hoffman, Margaret, 113

Idle Class, The, 33, 75, 79, 140
Immigrant, The, 14, 51, 56-57, 59
Ingram, Joan, 126
In the Park, 32, 55

James, Henry, *The Ambassadors*, 125
Jamison, Bud, 133
Jitney Elopement, The, 35
Joyce, James, 143
Joyce, Peggy Hopkins, 82

Karno, Fred, 12-14, 35
Kaye, Danny, 37, 145
Keaton, Buster, 39, 122, 125
Kelly, Hetty, 14, 17, 139
Kennedy, Merna, 91, 94, 135
Keystone Comedies, 14, 24-33
Keystone Kops, 24
Kids, The, 17, 33, 45, 69, 71, 72-74, 76, 79,
    141
Kid Auto Races at Venice, 14, 24
King in New York, A, 21, 125-128, 135, 137
Knock on Wood, 145
Knockout, The, 31
Knott, Lydia, 84
Korda, Alexander, 107

Laughing Gas, 27, 35
Laurel and Hardy, 145
Lehrman, Henry, 25

Liberty Bond Drive, 65, 67
Limelight, 21, 120, 121-125, 135, 137, 138, 141, 145, 147
Linder, Max, 143
Lloyd, Harold, 92n., 97, 143
Loren, Sophia, 129, 130, 131
Love Pangs, 26
Lubitsch, Ernst, 87
Lucas, E.V., 17
Ludwig, Emil, 132

Macdonald, Dwight, 115
McGranery, James, 21
Mabel at the Wheel, 29
Mabel's Busy Day, 31
Mabel's Married Life, 27
Mabel's Strange Predicament, 24, 35
Making a Living, 24, 25
Mann, Hank, 99
Marriage Circle, The, 87
Marx Brothers, 145
Medwin, Michael, 129
Melba, Nellie, 15
Menjou, Adolphe, 84, 85, 86
Miller, Carl, 82, 83, 85, 88
Modern Times, 19, 103-107, 108, 111, 128, 142, 145
Monsieur Verdoux, 21, 113, 115-119, 121, 123, 125, 137, 143, 145, 146
Mueller, Raquel, 97
Murray, Tom, 87
Myers, Harry, 96, 99, 100

Nash, Marilyn, 113, 118
Nathan, George Jean, 132
New Janitor, The, 33, 37, 49
Night at the Show, A, 35, 41
"Night in an English Music Hall, A," 14, 35
Night Out, A, 35
Nijinsky, Vaslav, 15, 67

Niklaus, Thelma, 111, 132, 133
Normand, Mabel, 24, 29, 31, 33

Oakie, Jack, 107, 112, 135
One A.M., 47, 50, 77
O'Neill, Eugene, 21
O'Neill, Oona (Mrs. Charles Chaplin), 20, 21, 121
On the Double, 145

Pavlova, Anna, 15
Pawnshop, The, 49, 53
Pay Day, 75, 77, 80
Payne, Robert, 132
Peter Pan, 12
Pickford, Mary, 15, 67
Pilgrim, The, 6, 17, 77, 79, 81, 138
Police, 39
Property Man, The, 35, 37
Purviance, Edna, 23, 36, 37, 43, 45, 49, 51, 52, 54, 56, 60, 61, 63, 65, 66, 67, 71, 72, 75, 77, 82, 83, 85, 88, 135

Raye, Martha, 113, 117, 119, 135
Recreation, 26
Riesner, Chuck, 43
Rink, The, 51, 55, 143
Robinson, Carl, 23
Rounders, The, 27, 35
Rutherford, Margaret, 131, 132

Seldes, Gilbert, 133
Sennett, Mack, 14, 29, 35, 49, 51
Shanghaied, 35
Shaw, George Bernard, 19, 138
Sherlock Holmes, 12
Shoulder Arms, 14-15, 65-67, 68, 70, 72, 73, 145
Sleeper, 145
Star Boarder, The, 29

Sterling, Ford, 24, 26
Sunnyside, 13, 67, 69, 71
Sutherland, Eddie, 43
Swain, Mack, 24, 26-27, 49, 75, 86, 90, 135

Tango Tangles, 29
Threepenny Opera, The, 119
Tillie's Punctured Romance, 30, 33
Tinney, Frank, 121
Totheroh, R.H., 43
Tramp, The, 37, 38, 39, 133, 143
Tree, Beerbohm, 15
Triple Trouble, 39
Turpin, Ben, 34, 35, 37
Twenty Minutes of Love, 26

Ulm, Gerith von, 133

Vagabond, The, 45, 46, 48, 54, 110
Vanderbilt, Mrs. William K., 15

Waite, Malcolm, 135, 136
Waugh, Evelyn, 138
Welles, Orson, 113
Wells, H.G., 17, 19
White, May, 41
Wilde, Oscar, 138
Woman of Paris, A, 17, 82-88, 90, 133n.,
    135n.
Wonder Man, 145
Work, 31, 35

Pyramid's Illustrated History of the Movies

a beautiful, original series of enchanting volumes on your favorite stars and motion pictures. Each book is superbly written and contains dozens of exciting photos! They are available from your local dealer, or you can use this page to order direct.

_____ **CHARLIE CHAPLIN** • Robert F. Moss • M3640 • $1.75 • The irrepressible Tramp known everywhere as a vastly comic and eloquent star.

_____ **BARBARA STANWYCK** • Jerry Vermilye • M3641 • $1.75 • Tough or sentimental, vicious or vulnerable, she was always the great actress.

_____ **EDWARD G. ROBINSON** • Foster Hirsch • M3642 • $1.75 • Unsurpassed for his vigorous, powerful performances in nearly ninety films.

_____ **SHIRLEY TEMPLE** • Jeanine Basinger • M3643 • $1.75 • The child star who sang, danced, smiled and pouted her way into the hearts of millions.

_____ **GRETA GARBO** • Richard Corliss • M3480 • $1.75 • The star who set the screen aglow with her beauty and artistry.

_____ **JOHN WAYNE** • Alan G. Barbour • M3481 • $1.75 • For nearly fifty years, the film's ideal of courage and "true grit".

_____ **CARY GRANT** • Jerry Vermilye • M3246 • $1.75 • An overview of this most popular star from the early years up through the 60's.

_____ **ELIZABETH TAYLOR** • Foster Hirsch • M3247 • $1.75 • The screen's most beautiful woman. Her films from a young girl to a foul-mouthed harridan.

_____ **SPENCER TRACY** • Romano Tozzi • M3248 • $1.75 • Sincere and honest, in private and before the public.

_____ **GANGSTERS** • John Gabree • M3249 • $1.75 • Raw violence and excitement over the last 40 years.

_____ **KARLOFF AND COMPANY: THE HORROR FILM** • Robert Moss • M3415 • $1.75 • Astute appraisal of the ghouls, ghosts and maniacs of the horror film.

_____ **BETTE DAVIS** • Jerry Vermilye • M2932 • $1.75 Vivid, flamboyant and thoroughly professional. An appraisal of her 80 films.

_____ **CLARK GABLE** • René Jordan • M2929 • $1.75 • Examination of his more than sixty films in which he reigned as "King of the Movies."

_____ **KATHARINE HEPBURN** • Alvin H. Marill • M2931 • $1.75 • A penetrating look at the enchanting comedienne and the brilliant dramatic actress.

_____ **HUMPHREY BOGART** • Alan G. Barbour • M2930 • $1.75 • A look at the man, the actor and the myth.

_____ **JUDY GARLAND** • James Juneau • M3482 • $1.75 • The electrifying singer who traveled "over the rainbow".

_____ **THE WAR FILM** • Norman Kagan • M3483 • $1.75 • The memorable films conveying all the brutality, courage and folly of war.

_____ **MARLENE DIETRICH** • Charles Silver • M3484 • $1.75 • The alluring enchantress with her unique aura of mystery and glamour.

_____ **JAMES STEWART** • Howard Thompson • M3485 • $1.75 • The ideal of warmth and sincerity during more than forty years of films.

_____ **W. C. FIELDS** • Nicholas Yanni • M3486 • $1.75 • The comic genius with the larger-than-life style and personality.

_____ **THE MOVIE MUSICAL** • Lee Edward Stern • $1.75 • From the dazzle and glitter of the thirties to today's widescreen opulence.

_____ **GARY COOPER** • René Jordan • M3416 • $1.75 • Moving portrait of America's most stalwart screen hero.

_____ **JOAN CRAWFORD** • Stephen Harvey • M3417 • $1.75 • Indomitable and vulnerable, Crawford has enchanted filmgoers for over four decades.

_____ **MARLON BRANDO** • René Jordan • M3128 • $1.75 • A look at the definitive screen "rebel", from the fifties to LAST TANGO.

_____ **MARILYN MONROE** • Joan Mellen • M3129 • $1.75 • Compassionate look at this deeply sensitive and very vulnerable woman.

_____ **INGRID BERGMAN** • Curtis F. Brown • M3130 • $1.75 • Extraordinary and stormy — a look at Bergman's more than forty films.

_____ **JAMES CAGNEY** • Andrew Bergman • M3127 • $1.75 • Ruthless gangster to nimble song-and-dance man.

_____ **PAUL NEWMAN** • Michael Kerbel • M3418 • $1.75 • The rebel, the renegade and the ruthless opportunist — a very sensitive analysis of a very popular actor.

Indicate the number of each title desired and **send this page** with check or money order to: **PYRAMID BOOKS**, Dept. MB. 9 Garden St. Moonachie, N.J. 07074

I enclose a check or money order for $_____, which includes the **total price** of the books ordered plus **50¢ additional per book** for postage and handling **if I have ordered less than 4 books. If I have ordered 4 books or more, I understand that the publisher will pay all postage and handling.**

MY NAME_____

ADDRESS_____

CITY_____

_____ STATE _____ ZIP _____

ABOUT THE AUTHOR

Robert F. Moss is an assistant professor of English at Rutgers University with a strong interest in film. He has published film criticism in *Film Heritage, Film Quarterly,* and *The New York Times.* He is also the author of the entry on film in the *Harper's Encyclopedia of the Modern World* and the *Encyclopedia of American History.* Another book to his credit is *Karloff and Company: The Horror Film,* published by Pyramid.

ABOUT THE EDITOR

Ted Sennett is the author of *Warner Brothers Presents,* a tribute to the great Warners films of the Thirties and Forties, and of *Lunatics and Lovers,* on the long-vanished but well-remembered "screwball" comedies of the past. He is also the editor of *The Movie Buff's Book* and has written about films for magazines and newspapers. He lives in New Jersey with his wife and three children.